T0344256

LEONARD, MARIANNE, AND ME

LEONARD, MARIANNE, AND ME

Magical Summers on Hydra

JUDY SCOTT

Backbeat
Books

Guilford, Connecticut

Backbeat Books

An imprint of The Rowman & Littlefield Publishing Group, Inc.
4501 Forbes Blvd., Ste. 200
Lanham, MD 20706
www.rowman.com

Distributed by NATIONAL BOOK NETWORK

British Library Cataloguing in Publication Information available

Library of Congress Cataloging-in-Publication Data available

Names: Scott, Judy, 1946- author.
Title: Leonard, Marianne, and me : magical summers on Hydra / Judy Scott.
Description: Lanham : Backbeat, 2021. | Includes index.
Identifiers: LCCN 2020052212 (print) | LCCN 2020052213 (ebook) | ISBN
   9781493059768 (cloth) | ISBN 9781493059775 (epub)
Subjects: LCSH: Cohen, Leonard, 1934-2016—Friends and associates. | Scott,
   Judy, 1946- | Ihlen, Marianne. | Hydra Island (Greece)—Description and
   travel. | Hydra Island (Greece)—Social life and customs.
Classification: LCC ML410.C734 S36 2021 (print) | LCC ML410.C734 (ebook)
   | DDC 782.42164092/2—dc23
LC record available at https://lccn.loc.gov/2020052212
LC ebook record available at https://lccn.loc.gov/2020052213

∞™ The paper used in this publication meets the minimum requirements of American National Standard for Information Sciences—Permanence of Paper for Printed Library Materials, ANSI/NISO Z39.48-1992

For George Lialios

Without your kindness and generosity,
none of this would have happened

CONTENTS

PREFACE

Most of us can point to a period, or event in our lives, and describe it as "seminal." For me, it was my discovery of the artist colony on the Greek island of Hydra in 1973. I met so many interesting, talented people during my first summer there who have had an important impact on my life up to the present. And the one who had the most impact was the incredibly talented literary and musical genius Leonard Cohen.

When asked in early 2016 to join with a number of other Hydra-related writers and artists in a literary project featuring our recollections of our experiences there, I knew what I had to do. Because the only thing Leonard asked of me, when he offered me his friendship and hospitality, was: "Promise you won't write about us."

So, on April 11, 2016, I sent him the following email:

Dear Leonard,

Greetings again, hope you and yours are well. My daughter, Victoria, who was started on Hydra 40 years ago, just bore my first grandchild, a boy, a joy!

Many years ago, you welcomed me for a brief time into your little Hydra family, and asked just one thing in return, "please don't write about us." And I have honored that request for over 40 years. But now, I have been invited to join with some other Hydra ex-pats, in a compendium of sorts, on our individual and shared experiences during the sixties, seventies, and eighties.

I had been working on a memoir for quite some time, and I don't really know if I want it to be included in this project or perhaps do something on my own with it. But first, I would seek your blessing.

There are some quite intimate and personal recollections. Some of it refers to things you may not even be aware of—particularly the parts about Suzanne and the children from my sojourn there in 1975. And some of it you may find disturbing. I would never want to violate the promise I made to you so long ago when you were incredibly kind to me, as was Marianne. If you can find a little time, I would be so edified if you could look it over and perhaps let me know your thoughts or if you have objections/edit requests.

Hydra and the brief time we all spent there together still hold a very loving place in my thoughts and my heart.

All good things,

Judy Scott (see attached)

To my surprise and delight, he wrote back the very next day. Leonard thanked me for sending him "this very fine piece of work for which I have no objections whatsoever." He mentioned that he was "very surprised" by some of what I'd written yet gratified to read about "so many of our old friends." He praised the "detail and honesty of the piece."

I decided not to join with the other Hydra-related writers but to write something more substantial of my own—something more in-depth.

I hope you enjoy reading it as much as I did living it.

—Judy Scott

Prologue

2003

I returned to the Greek island of Hydra again last night. The hydrofoil took a long time to get there this time—over two hours. I think it was partly because the sea was very rough for September. Of course, Monika was with me, as she has been for the past twenty years and something like ten trips here. We met our old friends, Brian Sidaway and his wife, Valerie, in the port and arranged for the donkey lady to take our bags up to the house we always rented from them.

It was a beautiful, fully-restored, authentic Greek cottage nicknamed "Poet's Corner." The donkey lady charged twice the going rate because it was after dark. They always charged foreigners more—we're pretty used to it.

Then we took the old familiar walk along the harbor front and stopped at the Sailing Café. We immediately spotted Yorgo, the short, rotund owner of the place. His eyes lit up when he saw us, and he greeted us warmly with the traditional European two-cheeked kisses.

"Ah, you are here again," he said. I've known Yorgo for almost thirty years.

When I first lived on Hydra in 1973 and again in 1975, Yorgo and his two siblings ran a little taverna just off Donkey Shit Lane called Three Brothers. It was one of the few restaurants that stayed open all winter long. The other one, up Kalo Pigadi (another main lane in the middle of town, whose name means "the good wells"), was Lulu's. All the foreigners would alternate between those two places for most of the winter months. Lulu's is still there, but Three Brothers was not so lucky. Alas, besides not being very good cooks, they were also not very good businessmen.

Yorgo doesn't know my name—I don't think he ever did. I doubt he remembered where I came from, but he remembered my face and was always happy to see me again. Yorgo is a very sweet man, especially for a Greek: kind and gentle—in my experience, these aren't typical Greek male qualities. Though, these days, Yorgo's smile is tinged with a world-weary sadness; in addition to the downturn in tourism, there was the death ten years ago of his oldest son in a terrible motorcycle accident in Athens and, just afterward, the death of one of his brothers who poisoned himself by mistaking a bottle of turpentine for a bottle of retsina. To be fair, the tree resin-infused Greek wine retsina does taste similar to turpentine. By the time Yorgo's brother realized his error, he'd chugged the whole bottle, and it was too late to save him.

"Next lifetime," said Yorgo, pointing to the large yachts in the harbor, "I will have one of those. Not a small one, but a very big one. Next lifetime."

Then he smiled again as we sat down to have a beer.

We'd spent the day in Athens after landing in Greece the night before. It was too late when we arrived by plane to connect directly to the hydrofoil. But it'd been a long time since I had spent any time in the city, so I didn't mind.

I called my friend George Lialios from the hotel in the evening, and we arranged to meet him and his German wife, Angelika, in Kifissia, a wealthy Athens suburb where they now lived. George was the first person I became friends with more than thirty years ago when I first arrived here.

I think about that time now as I sip my beer. I had no idea the turn my life was about to take. I was about to meet scores of interesting people. Lifelong friendships were soon to be forged.

Among them was Leonard Cohen and Marianne Ihlen.

Already, the island of Hydra was seducing me.

Passion.

Poetry.

Love.

I felt it the instant I set foot on the rocky isle.

I still feel it.

1

1973 AND 1974

It was early May. I'd just passed my twenty-seventh birthday. I was staying in a student pensione in Athens after hitchhiking through Ireland, England, Holland, France, Italy, and, finally, Greece. I'd initially come over with a cousin—but he had his brother's wedding he wanted to attend, so he flew back home from Athens, and I was once again on my own, ready for a solo adventure.

The pensione was just off Academia Street, one of the main thoroughfares in the heart of the city. Some of the people with whom I was traveling had gone out and bought *baklava* (as they couldn't find cake) and put a candle on it for me. An off-key version of "Happy Birthday" was sung amidst prodigious consumption of cheap white wine.

I'd met my traveling companions at the youth hostel in Kondokali on the island of Corfu: two Australian sisters in their mid-twenties who were doing their world tour; a lawyer named John from Chicago; and another American guy whose name I can't remember. They were all keen to visit another island, and I agreed as long as it was close by. I wasn't anxious for another overnight ferry ride.

John went off to research which islands were accessible within a few hours from Athens. He came back and announced he'd found the perfect trip: the island of Hydra, one of the Saronic Gulf Islands known to be an art colony of sorts. It was said to be filled with all kinds of itinerant foreign writers and artists—and it was the only Greek island that had no cars.

We all agreed that it sounded ideal.

The next day, we took the ferry. There were no hydrofoils in those days, and the ferry took three-and-a-half hours to reach the island. Pulling into port was an incredible sight. Hydra is one of the most beautiful and most famous islands in Greece—probably in the whole world, for that matter. The main town is built around three steep hills to the left, right, and behind a horseshoe-shaped, deep-water yacht port. It's not a very big island, at only eleven miles long and three miles wide, and the total population in those days was about three thousand, including around three hundred foreigners.

But it was a very special place, as I would come to discover.

The writer Henry Miller visited there during World War II, staying with his friend, Ghika, the internationally known Greek artist. Miller wrote a lovely and very appropriate description of Hydra in his Greek travelogue *The Colossus of Maroussi*: "Hydra is like the pause in a musical composition that allows the composer to proceed in a new direction. After Hydra, it is no longer about the destination, it's all about the path."

We found a small portside pensione and paid for three nights. The others wanted to pay for four, but I was anxious to move on to Istanbul, which was our next destination, so I convinced them to pay for only three. I reasoned that if we wanted to stay the extra night, there'd be no problem because the pensione was pretty much empty.

My plans all changed two days later, however, when I met George Lialios for the first time. We'd all been swimming and diving from the rocks. There were no beaches close to the main town, just stairs and ladders built into the side of the cliffs that led to a series of flat rocks and cement platforms from which one could dive into the beautiful blue water. After several hours of swimming and sunbathing, I left my friends and walked to the local taverna, then called Gregori's, in Kamini, the small fishing village to the west of the main town of Hydra, to use the bathroom and buy myself a beer. I sat outside on the quay to have my drink and was greeted by a neighboring table of lunchtime tourists.

At least I thought they were tourists, speaking French and all, but it turned out that one of them, George, was Greek and owned a very large house on the island—a mansion really—and the others were all his houseguests.

Back then, I probably looked as good as I've ever been in my life: tanned, curly-haired, short but well proportioned with good teeth, green eyes, and an Irish-bred pug nose. They invited me to join them, and before I knew it, I was being fork-fed roasted fish by George while Helga, his Austrian friend, rubbed her foot against mine under the table. *Holy shit,* I thought, *these may just be the decadent European rich people I've always heard about.*

After we finished our long and leisurely lunch, they invited me to accompany them up to George's house for a drink and a view of the sunset from his terrace. I thought I'd died and gone to heaven and quickly accepted. I had my beach bag with me containing my button-down collared, white cotton shirt (there are some things a Catholic schoolgirl never outgrows), a pair of cut-off jeans, and my newly purchased Greek sandals. We walked for what seemed like hours (it was actually only about twenty minutes), up and up and up four-hundred-plus steps to George's house. All the roads on Hydra have steps in them, which is why there's no wheeled transport on the island. No cars, no motorbikes, and no bicycles even. Just donkeys, boats, and feet.

Once we arrived at George's house, he set me up in his cavern-ous living/dining room with a glass of white wine (*Now you're talking!*), and the bathers all went off to take showers, leaving me sitting alone to examine the incredible home.

A short time later, the Greek housekeeper, Angeliki, answered a knock at the door, and in walked a lovely blonde Norwegian woman who introduced herself to me as Marianne. She pronounced her name in the Norwegian fashion with an accent on the final "e" (Mari-AN-ah) and joined me in the living room. She poured herself a glass of wine and sat down to chat, telling me that she'd come up the hill from her house because George, in those days, had one of the few telephones on the island, and she needed to make a call. She told me she'd lived on Hydra off and on for the better part of twelve years. Marianne (her last name was Ihlen) had lived there with a singer. "But that's all over now," she said kind of wistfully. "If I hadn't driven him crazy, he probably would not have written a thing. Perhaps you know him—Leonard Cohen?"

Oh, Jesus.

Leonard Cohen.

She was *that* Marianne.

"So Long, Marianne" Marianne.

Written and sung by one of my all-time favorite singer/songwriters. For ease of rhyme, the song might be titled "So Long, Marianne"— but to everyone, including Leonard, the name was always pronounced Mari-AN-ah (Marianne). Her married name had been Jensen, but then she took the last name of Cohen while she and Leonard were together. Now she was back to her maiden name: Ihlen. In the song "So Long, Marianne" (he'd altered her actual name to fit syllabically), there is a line—"I see you've gone and changed your name again"*—which references that fact.

Suddenly, this island just got a whole lot more interesting.

Yes, I'd heard of him; Leonard Cohen was, in fact, one of my idols. I had all his albums and knew all his songs by heart. I laughed and said,

---

* "So Long, Marianne," Leonard Cohen.

"Oh, my God, of course, I've heard of him—I think he's an incredible talent."

Marianne smiled, shook her head ruefully, and said, "We lived together for eleven years, but that's all over. He's back in Montreal now with another woman and a son who is two."

She looked away at that admission and grew quiet—remembering, it seemed.

Then the rest of the guests and George came back into the living room, and after another glass of wine and more conversation, Marianne completed her phone call and got up to leave. I walked with her through two antechambers (where two huge wine barrels, a bunch of cleaning-supply shelves, and a large refrigerator were stored) to the front door where she turned to me and said, "Come and visit me at my house. George can show you where it is."

"I think I'm leaving tomorrow," I replied.

Marianne slowly looked me up and down as if doing an internal evaluation and said, "Don't leave so soon, this is really a special place, you'll see. Stay awhile."

Later that evening, George invited me to move up to his house.

"I'm doing some painting in two of the bedrooms, and if you want to help me with that, you can stay here—no charge," he said.

He was about forty-five years old then, bald and very tanned. And you couldn't live on Hydra in those days, or even now, without being pretty fit from the climb back and forth from the port. His house was probably the nicest one I'd ever been in—seventeen rooms, including a huge ballroom with marble floors and thirty-foot-high ceilings. I was tempted. I asked if I could let him know the next day.

I decided to tell my traveling buddies that I probably wasn't going on to Istanbul with them after all.

The next morning, I saw George and Marianne sitting outside Tasso's café on the port and asked him if his offer was still good. He seemed pleased that I was going to join him. It turns out I'd been right about only paying for three nights at the harbor pensione after all.

That evening I packed my knapsack and climbed up Donkey Shit Lane for the first time. I spent the fourth night at George's house in my own bedroom with two big casement windows, a single bed, a dresser, and a little marble fireplace. I couldn't have guessed back then that I would climb those four hundred steps thousands of times in the years to come.

In the end, I never did help George with the painting, but I did keep him company while *he* painted, and he seemed perfectly happy with that. As they say, timing is everything, and for me, it was more than fortuitous. George enjoyed having company, and his friends were leaving the day after I arrived, so I fit the bill. Besides wall painting, George had all kinds of remodeling plans. He'd bought the house ten years earlier. It was built in the 1800s and had once belonged to a wealthy sea captain but had been abandoned for a long time and needed much work.

One of our most interesting early adventures—I like to call it "The Pink-Splotch Caper"—happened the following week when I accompanied George to Athens to pick out tiles for the bathroom. Whenever he went into the big city, George had a place to stay at the home of his good friend John Zervos. John was half British on his mother's side and half Greek on his father's side. He'd started a school called The Athens Centre, offering six- to eight-week courses in Greek culture, history, language, politics, and so on to college and university students from the United States for which they'd receive credits at their own institutions.

John lived at the time with Rosemary Donnelly, a girl from New Jersey (like me). They had a nice house in the Pangrati section of Athens behind the Acropolis and just above the old amphitheater, up the hill from the House of Parliament. Across the street from them and a little further up the hill was a place rented by a bunch of expatriates from several different countries. They'd all gotten together and chipped in to rent this big, old, four-bedroom house, which they used as a home base in their European travels. Things in Athens were very cheap in those days. I think they each paid the equivalent of fifteen US dollars a month, and there were about ten of them, but they didn't all stay there at the same time. George knew them too, and we went over to say hello right after we arrived.

It was after dark, and John warned us something dramatic had recently happened in this house. It involved Rosemary's brother, Jim, who was also traveling around. He'd recently returned from Nepal (in those days, everyone wanted to go to Kathmandu) where he and an American girl named Carol had journeyed together. She'd been living in Greece for several years with her (now former) boyfriend Marvin, a Jewish lawyer from Chicago. They'd even purchased a house together on the island of Paros. Apparently, Marvin had recently got wind of the fact that Carol was back in town and, needless to say, was still pretty upset about her dumping him. Anyway, we went across the street to hear Carol's story.

Carol greeted George with a kiss, shook my hand, and brought us into the big, wide kitchen that had twelve-foot-tall, side-by-side windows with a beautiful view of the Acropolis. We had some wine, and looking around the room, I noticed this large, splotchy pink stain on the wall of the whitewashed kitchen. Carol told us that when she and Jim got back to Athens, her ex, Marvin, wanted her to go with him to their island house "to settle up and get some of her things." But she was a little suspicious and said, "Uh-uh." So, for him, it was on to Plan B. He went around Athens one day, not long after she'd returned, and told some of their mutual friends whom he bumped into that he was going to kill her.

No one had cell phones in those days, and though the house she was staying in did have a landline, no one tried calling to warn her because no one really believed him. So, he showed up at the house around one a.m. that night and told Carol he wanted to speak with her. Into the kitchen they went—this very kitchen. In fact, she'd sat in the very chair in which I was now sitting. And as luck would have it, because it was dark out, those two beautiful, twelve-foot windows became like mirrors and reflected back the image of old Marvin hoisting a hatchet over his head and aiming it at Carol's. In a split second, she ducked and instinctively grabbed the back of her head. The blow glanced off her hand. She jumped up and started screaming and tried to run out of the room, but Marvin grabbed her and began banging her now-bleeding head against the wall (hence the pink splotch).

They were about the same height, so he wasn't getting anywhere with this Plan-B killing thing, and quite quickly, the other members of the household, awakened by the screaming, came running into the kitchen. In the confusion, Marvin dashed out the door and disappeared into the night. They later learned that he'd rushed to his apartment, packed his bags, and headed to Hellinikon Airport (back then the main hub servicing Athens). There, he inquired about the next flight to the United States but then had a change of heart and turned himself in to the airport police. Clearly, he was not thinking straight. He was taken to the Athens police headquarters, but once they ascertained that the person he'd attacked was not Greek (or dead), they let him go! This was very typical of Greek police in those days—they couldn't have cared less about foreigners unless they were rich tourists, and even then, not so much. So off he went to the airport once more, and this time, he scored a flight back to the Untied States. But, not ready to let bygones be bygones, Marvin phoned the house the next day, asked to speak with Carol, and warned her: "This is not over." (Actually, it was.)

As a postscript, once they knew he was safely far away in Chicago, they went out to the house on Paros and discovered that he'd dug a grave under the kitchen floor in preparation for her body. Carol seemed amazingly unfazed about all of this. George and I commiserated with her as best we could, finished our wine, and then went back across the street.

John and Rosemary had two low couches covered with flokati rugs opposite one another in their living room, and that's where we spent the night. Around three a.m., the resident cat must've been bothering George because I heard him whisper fiercely, "Get out. Get out of here!" And I thought, *Wow—a Greek man, talking to a Greek cat, in the middle of the night, in Athens . . . and he's speaking English!*

Several days later, George took me to meet his astrologer, Anita, who was apparently quite well known. As we walked up to her house, we crossed paths with a very stylish middle-aged woman who was on her way out.

George asked me, "Have you heard of Hermann Hesse?"

"Yes, of course," I replied. "I've read a few of his books."

"Well, that was his daughter-in-law. She comes here frequently, all the way from Germany. Anita is her astrologer, too."

Anita was a Swiss-German woman of about seventy. She and her Greek husband, Dimitri, lived by a kind of bog so close to Hellinikon Airport that one had to stop talking every time a plane took off or landed—it was that noisy. Their house, which they shared with twenty-three cats and three dogs, was old and wide open and, in a tub in the front yard, was a sea turtle they'd rescued from some children who'd caught it near the Piraeus harbor. The turtle had a large gash in its neck caused by capture, and Anita and Dimitri were planning on releasing it back to the sea once its wound healed. They were both dedicated animal lovers, and all their pets had been rescued at one time or another.

We'd brought a bottle of wine with us, and after introductions, glasses were produced.

Then George asked Anita if she would do my horoscope. She very graciously agreed, so I gave all my birth information to Dimitri. He wrote it down and went off to his office to prepare the chart. When he brought it back to Anita, she studied it very diligently for several minutes, nodding and jotting down notes.

"You have had some serious problems with your parents, both of them, but more so with your mother," Anita told me. "But you will overcome that. The bigger challenge is to find your place in this world. What you have is not just for one person. It is for many people, and that may not be easy for you to handle."

I was a bit dismayed by this revelation.

I asked her, "Does this mean I'll never have a permanent relationship, never get married or have a child?"

"Not necessarily," she replied, "but you will go through many steps and many challenges before you achieve any resolution." She also noted that I was a double Taurus (sun and moon) so that changes were not easy for me to accept. "Tauruses," she chuckled, "are notoriously stubborn. You must learn to be more flexible and, for a Taurus, that is a hard lesson." The one saving grace in my chart, according to Anita, was that I had Sagittarius rising. I had to laugh when she said that. It reminded me of one of my favorite lines from *The Catcher in the Rye*; it was on a note Holden found in his sister Phoebe's room: "You told me you were a Sagittarius, but you're only a Taurus!"

When we left, later that evening, George told me it was a real honor to have Anita read my chart, something she normally charged a good deal of money for. Then he asked me about my relationship with my parents.

I told him about the most recent time I'd seen my father, who was a serious alcoholic, somewhat of a town drunk. It was the previous winter. My parents had been separated for over eight years. Both of them had moved back to Kearny, New Jersey, the town where I was born. My mother had found a job in personnel at Congoleum Nairn, the same company that my father's father had moved from Scotland to work for. In 1910, Lord Nairn had brought a bunch of young workers with him when he immigrated to America and set up his factory, making linoleum rugs and flooring which, I guess, were very popular furnishings in the early twentieth century.

Anyway, after my parents separately moved back to their home-town, my father got a job as a janitor for the Prudential Insurance Company in Newark, New Jersey, but he didn't keep any job for long because of his drinking. Raising my two much younger sisters was really hard on my mother because she could never count on getting any child support from him.

I'd long since abandoned their fraught relationship and moved to Los Angeles to attend college and escape the emotional damage they caused one another and anyone else in the mix. But every Christmas and summer vacation, I always journeyed back to New Jersey to spend the holidays "at home."

One day in early January, while I was still there, I heard the sound of my father snoring in the basement under Mom's first-floor apartment. The owners, an older, retired Polish couple, lived up on the second floor of the two-family house. *Oh shit*, I thought.

He was sleeping in the cellar where there were several rolled-up carpets but no bed. I knew I'd have to get him out of there before my mother got home from work. I paced up and down the flat, listening to his heavy breathing noises until I couldn't wait any longer, knowing she'd be back at any moment. I went down there and, after tugging on his arms several times, finally managed to wake him up.

"You have to go," I told him. "You can't stay here."

He sat up, and in the dim light of the cellar bulb, I could see a stream of dried blood streaking his forehead and cheek. It was bitter cold out, and the streets and sidewalks were covered in ice. I figured that he must have slipped and fallen and cut his face.

"I don't have any place to go," he told me, and I silently cursed the fact that I was being dragged back into this endless domestic drama. But I knew that if I didn't get him to leave, there'd be a huge scene. Possibly the landlords would get involved and, who knew, maybe even the police as well.

"You can't stay here, Dad," I said. "You have to leave right now."

I gave him ten dollars, all the cash I had on me, and watched him slowly climb the stairs and disappear into the freezing cold night. That much I told George.

For months afterward, when I'd returned to Los Angeles, I worried it might have been the last time I'd ever see my father, but it wasn't, thank heavens. In later years, I saw him periodically. By then, he'd been in and out of the Veterans Hospital and was living in a kind of flophouse hotel in Kearny. I'd arranged for his social security check to be deposited in my bank account, and I'd go down from New Milford, where I was living with my sister, and pay the local deli in Kearny to give him food every day. I also bought him some new clothes, and for a time, he seemed to be doing quite well.

But one day a few months later, he telephoned me, completely drunk, and said, "I need help." Someone whom I did not know got on the line and said, "You need to come and get your father. He's in bad shape." My father was fifty-seven at the time.

During World War II, he'd seen heavy action in the Pacific theater as a tail-gunner on a B-29 bomber. His plane was badly shot up during one raid, barely managing to limp back to their home base on Saipan. Dad was awarded the Distinguished Flying Cross and six Air Medals and left the Army Air Corps as a staff sergeant. But he was never able to stop the panic attacks or the drinking he resorted to in order to block out those memories. My great-aunt Anna, with whom he had lived for a while, probably got it right when she made the following observation: "It was the war that ruined them."

The day after that phone call, I contacted the VA Hospital where he'd been treated in the past, and the really nice man on the other end of the line told me, "Don't ask if you can bring him in; just bring him."

And so I did. I picked him up, with all his worldly belongings packed in a large black garbage bag, and took him to the VA Hospital in Lyons, New Jersey, and that's where he lived for the next fifteen years.

And that's where he died.

So, to hear this astrologer zero in on my relationship to my parents—which is to be expected, that's how astrologers work, homing in on the relationships closest to our heart—it struck a bit of a nerve. I would be processing what she said for the next few days. She'd specifically singled out my mother—but the more troubling issues and resentments obviously revolved around my father.

George and I returned to the island the next afternoon, catching the ferry at two. Already, I couldn't wait to return to Hydra. It cost about three dollars in those days. We bought a third-class ticket but went into the first-class lounge. George knew all the workers on the ship, including the captain. George had lived on Hydra for about fifteen years at this point, so he'd taken these ferry rides many times and always bought a third-class ticket but then rode in first class. The difference was only about a dollar, but it was a "privilege" issue, according to George. He was from an old, wealthy Greek family. Letting us into first class was a sign of respect, he told me. I ran into Marianne and her young son, Axel, at the port several times during the first two weeks of my stay. She always encouraged me to drop by, but I was having such a wonderful time reading, sunbathing, and drinking beer on George's terrace overlooking the whole island that I put off most visits unless I was accompanying George someplace. I felt it was kind of my obligation to keep him company since he was being so kind and generous and didn't even try to sleep with me or anything.

I also got to meet many interesting people—all of George's friends. Hydra was (and still is) an art colony, so most of the people I met were artists, writers, and musicians. They were all welcoming. Knowing George was a big help, and so was the fact that, in May, the season hadn't really started and new faces were at a premium.

Even old Madame Pauori got wind of my arrival and sent me an invitation to one of her famous luncheon salons. She'd been on Hydra for a very long time. Her picture, with Hydra in the background, was actually on the back of the Greek thousand-drachma note. Most people on the island knew that—but they didn't know the deeper story: The government mint had used Pauori's face as the model for Boubulina, the female heroine of the Greek revolution against the Turks. Boubulina had led several naval battles successfully with a fleet of vessels built and launched from Hydra (though she herself was from the next island, Spetsi).

Madame Pauori was no longer the raving beauty of the banknote. She was fairly old and quite rich. She had a huge house—a pink palace, really—on the left side of the port. Her guest book was impressive: Henry Miller, Sophia Loren, Melina Mercouri, Jules Dassin, Audrey Hepburn, John Lennon and Yoko Ono, Allen Ginsberg, Gregory

Corso, Pablo Picasso . . . lots of other famous Americans, Europeans, and Greeks, most of them from the artistic, literary, and entertainment fields. She showed me all the notable signatures and insisted I sign her book, too. She'd heard I might be doing some writing, and she didn't want to take any chances—someday I might be famous too.

George loved to hear about my dreams. I've always had very vivid ones, and I've always been able to recall them the next morning. Truth be told, my dreams were much more creative and interesting than anything I said or did in waking life. So, every morning, we'd have coffee with bread or toast and I'd tell George about my dreams from the night before. Then we'd go down to the port (again, over four hundred steps) to shop, see his friends, and sit and watch the show. And what a show it was.

Tourists came in on the day boats—tour boats that hit three islands, usually Poros, Hydra, and Spetsi, during a ten-hour trip. They'd disembark and run around the port looking in shops, buying souvenir bangles, postcards, or worry beads, and sit and eat elaborate, extremely over-priced ice cream and fruit sundaes. Oh, and they'd take donkey rides, straddling the big, wooden saddles that all natives rode sidesaddle while all the tourists rode like in the Old West. They'd take pictures of one another with their donkeys and traverse the backstreets of the main town. Lots of them, even back then, were Japanese. We'd watch them and wait for the big blast of the ship's horn, warning them it was time to depart. There were always a couple of stragglers who'd go flying through the port, waving and shouting to the boat to wait for them. And sometimes, there were a couple of hapless visitors left behind. The Greeks, in general, may not be great when it comes to promptness, but the tour boats and ferries were not kidding around. They were very punctual, and if you weren't back when they said to be back, you were history.

And so, I passed a couple of blissful, serene weeks keeping George company, lying on his terrace, sipping my beer and reading. George had an excellent library with books written in all four languages that he spoke. It was the perfect spot to be introduced to *The Alexandria Quartet*.

George also gave me a copy of *Dianetics* to read. He and his close friend, Leonard Cohen, had become interested in Scientology some years before and even spent time in Copenhagen on author L. Ron Hubbard's ship. But they'd quickly grown disillusioned with the man and his theories and were no longer members or devotees by the time I came along. George did think there were some interesting observations in the book, however, and suggested I check it out. I found the book far-fetched and very boring. I just couldn't get through it. I told George that, as a philosophy major, I'd read and studied a number of different metaphysical theories on how the universe worked, and this one seemed nothing more than second-rate science fiction. George just shrugged and smiled. It didn't seem to bother him a bit.

George was very interested in all things spiritual. He wore a small, embossed silver amulet on his left bicep, tied with several strands of red cotton thread. The amulet contained a small piece of paper which had writing on it in Sanskrit. The message was a lesson. George was instructed to wear the amulet, never taking it off until all the threads had worn through. At that point, it would fall away, and the lesson, whatever it was, was assumed to have been learned. It'd been given to him by one of his teachers in India. George went there almost every winter and had met with many gurus and spiritual leaders. Years later, I became interested in one of those teachers, one named Babaji. On a later visit, I asked George if he had ever met with him, and he said yes. In fact, Babaji had invited him to stay at his ashram, but it wasn't George's scene, rather primitive and lacking music or books or any interesting sidelights, so George had declined the offer.

I had very limited interest in Indian gurus. Babaji died only about a year after I'd heard of him, and though I met some of his trusted advisors when they visited Los Angeles where I was living, I found them to be profoundly lacking in any sense of play or humor (though everyone said that Babaji himself was "very playful"). They seemed extremely taken with their own self-importance; in other words: boring.

Anyway, George taught me how to throw the *I Ching*. That was more my style, and I was quite impressed with how prescient some of its lessons were, especially the "moving lines." I still consult it every once in awhile, even to this day.

George and I discussed a myriad of ideas during this peaceful, pleasant period. One of the things I was most curious about was the indigenous population, the islanders, and George told me all about them. The Greeks on Hydra were all originally from Albania, he said. They'd fled the Turkish invasion and settled Hydra in the eighteenth century. Albanians were (and still are) notoriously xenophobic. On the other islands I visited, if one passed a Greek person on the road, they'd always greet you with *kali mera* (good day) or *yasou* (hello) and a big smile. George taught me his favorite greeting, and it's one I use even today: *hierete*.

It means rejoice.

On Hydra, however, none of the locals would ever initiate a greeting. If one acknowledged them first, they'd always politely reciprocate—but no smile, though.

When I first lived there, in 1973 and 1975, there were a number of people with congenital defects. George explained that up until the early sixties, very few Hydriots ever left the island. He said many only got as far as Athens and that was a big-deal visit, for a birthday perhaps or a marriage trip. Therefore, often when we went down to the harbor front, we'd see the son of the bakery owners running through the port, hands pounding his ears, silently screaming. No sound from his mouth, for he was a deaf-mute, but the grimace on his face betrayed a consciousness of inner agony and incurable pain of some kind. He didn't live very long past his adolescence, or so I heard.

And then there was Captain Yanni, a very gentle but brain-damaged man, who refused—even in wintertime—to wear anything on his feet. He could speak (in a child-like voice) but was not able to manage any kind of job. Townspeople, especially Kyria Sofia, who owned a taverna way up Kalo Pigadi, and Kyria Marigoula, who owned a small grocery store, took care of him as best they could. Whenever I saw him, he seemed happy in his own way. But as is often the case, poor Captain Yanni was frequently tormented and mercilessly teased by the island's young men, and eventually, to escape their taunts while visiting a Greeks-only café high above the harbor, he fell (or was pushed) backward onto the stone steps, hit his head, and died.

There was also a short, hunchbacked young woman who'd come down from the top of the hill where she lived with her family to do her shopping. I'm pretty sure she could speak, but I never heard her say anything, and she shied away from strangers, probably self-conscious about her deformity.

And then there was the crazy lady who lived in a capacious, abandoned house on the hill opposite George's. She'd come out at sunset to scream epithets to the entire island.

"Bastards!" she'd cry out in Greek. "Sons of bitches! Whores! You will all burn in hell!"

I later found out she was the mother of Philemon, a donkey man who was outgoing and affable with the foreigners. Philemon was a good friend of Anthony Kingsmill, the longtime resident British artist who was also a very close friend of Leonard Cohen. I knew Philemon pretty well, and though he was considered irascible and often very cranky, I got along great with him. He had two brothers in the Greek Merchant Marine. All three were heavy smokers and, at various times, contracted tuberculosis and died in their mid-forties. When I returned in 1982, Philemon and his mother were gone, and I still kind of missed them both.

Lastly, there was sweet Lefteris, who started out as a donkey man but later got a job in the bank where I would go to cash my traveler's checks. He had a congenitally deformed leg that he had to drag behind him as he made his wobbly way along the port. As a regular customer, I got to know him pretty well. He spoke English and was very friendly. Years later, he married a Swiss girl (or she might have possibly been Dutch), and they had a little daughter. I was so happy for him. When I ran into him during one visit, coming down the hill on his donkey, I congratulated him, and he beamed with pride.

The high incidence of birth defects in the island's native population was due to the depleted gene pool. There were only so many families on Hydra, and they'd been intermarrying for years and years. Very little new stock got introduced. There were rumors about other children born with serious deformities or very limited mental capacities who were kept hidden away and never allowed out of the house. But then there were also rumors about wild dogs roaming the hills and attacking people at night. Back in that time, the island Greeks hated dogs, and even their hunting dogs were kept in miserable conditions on short chains when not actually in use during hunting season. George was pretty sure both rumors were simply local myths.

Today things are very different. It's now fashionable to have dogs on Hydra, and for a while, they competed with the roosters to disturb everyone's sleep at night. However, since the avian flu epidemic, local by-laws were changed, and it's no longer permitted to keep poultry within twenty yards of a domicile or business for fear of scaring off the tourists. Houses are all very close together, so if anyone still has chickens and roosters, they must be kept way up on top of the hills where one can no longer hear them. Most of them, I'm pretty sure, ended up in a soup.

May 18, 1973, was Marianne's thirty-eighth birthday. George arranged to have a small dinner party for her at his house and invited several other ex-pats who lived on the island.

That evening, everything changed.

The American artist Jane Motley was there with her British boyfriend, Richard. So was Doctor Gordon, a gay American physician who wasn't very friendly. There were a couple of other people as well, but I don't recall them now. It seemed odd, but there were no other Greeks invited. The locals and ex-pats didn't socialize together very much, and since George was not from Hydra and rather wealthy, he gravitated more toward the foreigners.

That morning, George and I bought groceries in the port for the party and arranged to have them hauled uphill by donkey. That afternoon, we baked a cake. George cooked dinner for everyone: coq au vin, roasted vegetables, and a big salad with George's delicious garlic-and-mustard dressing. I put on the only dress I'd brought with me and told Marianne when she arrived that I seldom wore dresses (like, never) but wanted to do something special for her birthday. After dinner in the adjoining dining room, we all moved to the living room, and I sat down in front of the huge fireplace at a low table surrounded by little stools with cushions on them. Marianne sat just to my left on the built-in sofa.

While I was lighting the candles on her cake and everyone was watching this little common ceremony, I felt someone's hand caressing my ankle under the table. What the hell? It could only be one person—Marianne. I didn't look up or react in any way. I continued lighting the candles while the anonymous hand continued gently stroking my bare skin. I gave no acknowledgment, no sudden look of shock, no visible response whatsoever. In just such a way, I calmly continued moving the match across the cake, while inside my skull, my brain was exploding.

WOW, was all I could think. *What an incredibly brave thing to do.* To make an obvious (though hidden) pass at a virtual stranger in front of one's closest friends. And another female at that! How amazing to instinctively know it was safe (or maybe to just be fascinated by the risk involved), not to mention being an irresistible thing to do.

From that moment on, anything and everything I did on Hydra that summer revolved around Marianne. Aside from being very beautiful, Marianne had an incredibly attractive personality: warm, funny, engaging, and eternally curious about life, people, spiritual things, magic—the whole nine yards. And at the same time, during the course of the time I knew her, I found her to be magnificently manipulative. I never thought (well, OK, maybe once or twice) that anything she did in our relationship was intentional, strategic, or deliberately hurtful. She was just extraordinarily intuitive, almost feral when it came to keeping one off base and somehow dumbfounded, discombobulated . . . constantly wondering: *What the hell is going on?* Everything for Marianne seemed to operate at a subliminal level, yet she was able, with almost no exposure to herself, to keep all the people she was interested in (and over the years, there were quite a few) emotionally subjugated yet totally infatuated.

We spent a lot of time together after that, in her house . . . talking. She told me a great deal about her past, and I wanted to know everything. We shopped together, ate meals together (Marianne was a meticulous housekeeper and an excellent cook), went daily to the rocks to swim in the beautiful Aegean Sea, and spent time with her son, Axel, who was then thirteen, just hanging out.

One time, we went to the post office (when it was still up the steps on the second floor of the building at the left end of the port) and asked for her mail. The post lady recognized her, of course, and handed her three letters (I think one might have been a postcard). To my astonishment, they were all addressed the same way:

Marianne, Hydra, Greece

That was it. No last name, no address or Poste Restante, no other description. I wrote later in my diary: *I know they say no man is an island, but I know a woman who is one!*

And then, one day, not too long after that, Marianne was gone. Gone into Athens with no word to me, no warning, just gone. She'd only left a message for George (who knew nothing of this as-yet-only-emotional affair of mine) saying she was going to the city to conduct some business. Stunned by this turn of events, I was relieved when, several days later, George told me we needed to go into Athens again as well.

I was breathless at the idea that I could see Marianne again. And see her I did the next evening at a party given at the ex-pats' house across the street from John and Rosemary's. I couldn't wait for the party to begin, and when we finally arrived, Marianne was already there. She was talking to someone, I don't remember who, and I went to her side immediately and said, "Hi, we're here!"

She turned to me rather formally and said quite coldly, "Oh, hello, nice to see you again."

No embrace, no hug, no kiss, no real acknowledgment whatsoever.

I might just as well have been someone she'd met long before for a very brief time, someone she kind of recognized but couldn't quite place. She then turned her back to me and resumed her conversation. She didn't attempt to include me or introduce me to whoever was now absorbing her attention. It was like she'd erased me from memory. Where once I'd felt secretly embraced, now I felt publicly slapped in the face (not that anyone noticed—or had any idea that I'd just been emotionally crushed). I almost had to shake my head to try and clear it.

I wasn't yet quite accustomed to such abrupt emotional reversals. I looked around for someone else to talk to and, failing that (amazing to feel such utter solitude in a crowded party), went to the bar, got a glass of wine, turned, and watched her continue to completely ignore my existence.

The party was pretty crowded by then, and after a time, feeling no inclination toward shallow conversation with people I didn't know very well, I felt the need to escape. I told George I had a headache and was going back across the street to lie down. Of course, I did stop at the bar on my way out to refill my glass. Hey—happy times, sad times, lovely times, bad times . . . I was not going to be deprived of the consolation that a large glass of white wine could bring.

It was mid-summer in Athens, and as I crossed the street, the sun set over the Acropolis, easily visible in the distance. Dismayed though I definitely was, I still experienced (aside from some very raw emotions) the wonder, splendor, and sheer beauty of that moment. I was hurt, but I was *alive*. I let myself into the living room and sat on the flokati to consider my options.

I hadn't intended to spend a month in one place, and though I loved my new adopted island, I thought maybe it was time to move on. After all, I was a traveler, bent on seeing as many new countries, cities, sights as possible before I ran out of money. The problem was, all my stuff was back on Hydra, so I'd have to return with George to pack up my bruised ego and small knapsack before I could be off again.

I'd pretty much made up my mind that this was the only reasonable course of action when the front door opened and in walked Marianne.

This lady seemed to have an endless capacity to surprise me. I didn't know why, and I didn't know how, but I seemed to be, at least for the time being, the chosen one. We sat together and talked for hours. She never suggested going back to the party. Once again, I was the center of her attention—it made me happy. Around two in the morning, the party broke up, and the others returned to the house. Marianne left with a promise to meet the next day.

And we did meet the next day, and the one after that and the one after that. We returned to Hydra on the ferry later that week. In the meantime, John Zervos had arranged for some of his students at The Athens Centre to take Greek lessons in Athens in conjunction with the Greek American Union. He invited Marianne and me to attend for free, and so we did for a couple of days. Whatever Greek I now know (around a hundred words) came from those initial introductory lessons. Although Marianne had lived in Greece for a dozen years, she didn't have much aptitude for the language and only spoke at about my level. Me, I love languages and pick them up pretty quickly. I can now get by in Spanish, French, and Greek (forget German, though).

The day before we left Athens, Marianne told me she had to go down to the customs office in Piraeus. A friend of hers had sent a box of *Bidis* (Indian cigarettes), and they were being held in customs until the officials could conclude that there were no drugs in the package. Marianne told me she thought it was probably hopeless given the Greek mentality when it came to foreigners, but off we went anyway.

She presented the notice she'd received to the plump Greek man at the counter, and he led us back into a cavernous warehouse. He pointed to an old wooden desk and opened one of the drawers, and there were the *Bidis* in what resembled a cigar box. But no, we couldn't take them just yet. First, Marianne had to sign a release. So off they went, leaving me sitting behind the desk. I seriously considered slipping the box into my purse, but I then thought, *What if they come back with the release and the* Bidis *have disappeared?*

Well, my first instinct proved right because when they returned, Marianne motioned for me to follow her out the door. As we were leaving (sans *Bidis*), she told me they didn't have the lab report back from another bureau in Athens, and so they wouldn't let her take them. "I'm afraid it's hopeless," she said. "By the time they release them, they'll be totally stale and unsmokeable."

I think we spent about five days in Athens on that trip. Marianne was staying with a gay medical student named Spiro (if I remember correctly) with whom she was having a casual affair. He was from a wealthy Greek family that lived in Alexandria, Egypt. Spiro had an ex-boyfriend named Bill Finley, and I heard later that Finley and Marianne got into a big fight over Spiro at the café Apotsos, an unlikely "hot" spot that George took me to every time we were in Athens. Unlike Zonar's Café (where the local hoi polloi hung out), which was situated on a prominent corner of Academia Street, Apotsos was deliberately déclassé. Just off Academia Street, at the end of a small, dark arcade containing lots of jewelry shops, it was a classic Greek *ouzeria*. Filled with small marble tables, mismatched chairs, several display cases of *mezzedes* (comestibles), and any kind of alcohol one could imagine, it was minimally decorated with old advertising posters, yet it had become the "in" place to be. In fact, I went there many times on my numerous trips to Greece until, like so many things, the building got purchased and razed, and Apotsos was no more.

I later learned that W. H. Auden, the famous British poet, was also a patron there (as were a number of Members of Parliament). Auden, who was also gay, started out as a good friend of Finley's, but they ended up bitter enemies who would occupy adjoining tables at Apotsos with their respective *parea* (cliques) and glare at one another—a falling out over a boy, no doubt. I learned there was quite a bit of interaction between social groups at Apotsos and on Hydra. Finley actually rented a house on the island for a time, and people visited back and forth often.

Bill Finley was a notorious figure in Athens society who'd been in Greece for a long time. He knew everyone worth knowing in the ex-pat and literary crowd and was an "out" gay man when that was not considered very wise. He hadn't always been out or gay, though. In fact, he'd been married twice: once to a member of the Vanderbilt family, and once to a member of the Cunard (shipping line) family. Got to hand it to him, he had great taste.

Finley had also been friends with George Katsimbalis, who was immortalized as "The Colossus of Maroussi" by Henry Miller in Miller's book of that same name. I asked George Lialios once if he'd known Katsimbalis, as well, and he affirmed, "Yes, I did know him. He was very famous all around Athens back in the days just before the German occupation." I was so happy to realize, then, that I was only one degree of separation from the wild Greek of Miller's book and only two degrees separated from Henry Miller himself.

One evening, Spiro, Marianne, and I went out to a French restaurant in Kolonaki Square. I don't remember everything I ordered, but I do remember the deadly escargot. I'd been invited to sleep at Spiro's that night, so when we got back to his apartment around two a.m., I lay down on the couch in the large living room, and they curled up on a double mattress across the room from me. I was already feeling queasy when Marianne motioned for me to come over and join them. What a time to have food poisoning! I didn't want to disclose how sick I felt, so I just shook my head and turned over as if to sleep. As soon as I heard their soft, steady breathing, I got up quickly, made it to the bathroom, and puked my guts up.

Oh, Jesus, was I sick. Damn.

My first opportunity to spend the night in a bed with Marianne, and instead, I spent it hugging the porcelain throne.

So back we went the next morning to Hydra. Although it took over three hours by ferry, I loved those old ocean-going boats. My favorite was the biggest of the three that called each day to Hydra. It was named the *Portokalis Illios* (the Orange Sun). Now there are only hydrofoils. All the old boats have been taken out of service. And where once it cost three dollars by boat, it's now twenty-five dollars each way on the Flying Dolphins.

I was once asked what I thought had changed the most on Hydra in the thirty years I've been visiting. After some thought, I said hydrofoils and modern packaging. Hydrofoils allowed lots more people to come for weekend trips, whereas on the ferry, the seven-hour round trip discouraged them. And when I lived there, everything from the market was packaged in small gray paper bags or white butcher's paper. Garbage was burned in the fireplace.

Nowadays, since there are many more visitors coming to the island and many foodstuff items are prepackaged in plastic, the community has a terrible time keeping up with all the trash. Outside the main village, it litters the pathways, the ditches, the beach . . . urban blight eventually found its way to Hydra.

One day, early in my affair with Marianne, while we were sitting in her kitchen as per usual, she said to me: "You know, Judy, you're nothing like I imagined you to be."

I felt in an instant that I'd been found out. That I was discovered to be a fraud; not the cool and elusive being I tried to portray. That fatal hesitation. I knew I wasn't brave enough to ever dare to touch a stranger on the leg—and now Marianne knew it, too. But I only looked at her and asked: "What did you imagine me to be?"

"I don't know," she answered. "Just . . . different."

"Well, maybe I was just too easy."

She laughed then and shook her head.

"Let's have some more beer," she said.

It was only much later, years later, that I realized no one is ever as you first imagine them to be. The illusion of the magical other is eventually replaced by a real, living, breathing human being. It may take only a few brief encounters, or half a lifetime, but eventually, we recognize that we are all only people, after all.

George and I ate dinner out most nights, mostly at a taverna called Douskos. I always insisted on paying for my own meal and, after several more weeks there, money began to run low. I was very reluctant to leave now that Marianne and I were getting along so well (still nothing physical, though), but I made plans anyway to depart for Paris the following week.

Then Marianne got a phone message that once again changed everything: Leonard was coming.

"You can't leave now," Marianne said. "You have to stay and meet Leonard."

As if anything could have stopped me.

My three all-time favorite singers/songwriters/performers were Leonard Cohen, Van Morrison, and Willie Nelson. Leonard was unquestionably my number one.

I first discovered his songs via Judy Collins, whose singing I also loved (I saw her once in LA at the Troubadour, and Joni Mitchell was in the audience). I bought all her early albums, and that was how I was introduced to Leonard's incredible songs. Collins' album *In My Life* had the incomparable "Suzanne" as its lead track, and her album *Wildflowers* had two of my favorite of Leonard's early compositions: the beautiful

"Sisters of Mercy" and the incredible "Hey, That's No Way to Say, Goodbye." Those albums were released in 1966 and 1967, and it didn't take long after listening to her renditions for me to seek out and enjoy the man and his music. Since then, I've purchased everything he has released, and I even bought an album of his in Toronto, *Leonard Cohen: Live Songs* (1973), that was never released in the United States.

Leonard arrived the next day. I knew what time he was expected, and though Marianne had invited me to come by, I waited several hours before making an appearance. I was so excited to be meeting him, but I wanted to allow some time for the three of them to be together again by themselves. Finally, anticipation overcame discretion, and I left George's house, stopped at Four Corners to buy a nice bottle of wine, and breathed a sigh of relief when I found the downstairs entrance door open. I walked into the kitchen, and there he was, sitting casually at the big oak table. Marianne was cooking something on the little two-burner petrol gas stove just behind him. Leonard looked so at home; it seemed to me like he had never really left. He was back in his house, with his Hydra family, and all was well with the world.

Marianne turned around and introduced us. "This is my new, very best friend in the world," she said. "You're going to like her, she's very special, just don't try to steal her from me!" We all laughed at that, and Leonard got up and gave me a hug. "Welcome, it's very nice to meet you," he said.

I really thought I had died and gone to heaven, and in the days and weeks that followed, heaven would have been a poor substitute. I visited every day, and Leonard was always very friendly and engaging. And he always made a little time to sit and chat with me (and share a beer). Marianne did not seem to mind a bit that I became so ubiquitous in their house; in fact, we all got along great. Leonard and I spent a fair amount of time talking and then singing together. I wasn't very good at harmony, but I do have a fairly good voice, and Leonard seemed to enjoy having someone else to sing with. We also talked about music, about different styles. I asked him if he liked the Blues, and he said, "Yes, I do, but I've never really been able to play them well. On the guitar, it requires a lot of very quick fretting—and I'm not very good at that technique." He quickly ran through a couple of more-than-adequate Blues riffs to demonstrate.

"It's quite different from folk guitar," he said, "so I stick to that."

I told him I'd done a paper in my Phenomenology Class on the philosophical meaning of the Blues. He actually looked interested and asked me what I'd written. The Blues, I suggested, is the musical manifestation of the 1/32 of a second between when a sound emanates and when it's perceived. Science teaches us that it takes 1/32 of a second for a sound to be perceived by a given organism after it is made. It is that gap—that less-than-split-second gap—that keeps us out of the flow of existence. It's the expression not of existential dread exactly (as described by Albert Camus) but more like an exquisitely painful experience of separation: a singularity that defines each of us, but also isolates us from one another and from our world.

"That Blues music is often expressed as a wail or a cry," I explained, "that is easily perceived though not consciously understood. It's the anguish of recognition that we can never really be in the 'present.' It's the universal cry of exquisite solitude." (Or, as Jackson Browne so eloquently put it: "In the end there is one dance you'll do alone."*) "It easily defines each of us but also isolates us from one another and from our world."

Leonard considered that for a bit, then nodded.

---

* Browne's iconic song, "For a Dancer."

"That's a very interesting take on it, Judy," he said. "I like it. You could be right."

I discovered that, oddly, nobody on Hydra sang or played the Blues, even *Rebetika*—the Greek musical equivalent to American Blues music—was seldom heard or played on Hydra. The island somehow granted such a state of grace that the flow of existence seemed to be totally in sync with "the organism" in question. Something about the atmosphere itself—it made us all feel embraced and supported, not just part of a small but vibrant community of souls but also with existence itself. Some Hydra sycophants claimed the island was an "energy spot" on the Earth; that if one drew a straight line between two of the holiest places in Greece, Knossos, and Delphi, it would go right through Hydra. That may be true. I never looked it up. But there was something ineffable and visceral that kept us all there—or longing to be there, when we were away.

I remember walking barefoot over granite paving stones along the quay and harbor. There was a sensation of energy, of something emanating from below that was ineluctably pleasurable. And though the sun beat down insistently, the rocks never became unbearably hot, like sand at a beach does. The rocks on the many staircases that served as roads on Hydra, however, sometimes became so energized by the heat of the sun, that they were actually slippery. When running down the stairs, especially if wearing Greek leather-soled sandals, one had to be careful to set a foot in the middle of each step, or you'd slip and fall off the edge (how apropos).

During one of those lovely early weeks that I spent with George, before all the later drama and romantic complications, he and I were standing on his terrace drinking some white wine and watching the sun slowly sink into the Aegean Sea. We'd read earlier that day, in the *International*

Herald Tribune (a traveler's bible back then), that Jacqueline Kennedy Onassis was on the Onassis yacht visiting ports on the Peloponnese. It struck me that we were very likely watching the same sunset.

I said to George, "It doesn't really matter how much money you have or don't have, whether you're a millionaire or just a donkey man, does it George? You still get to experience exactly the same incredibly beautiful Greek sunset."

Leonard was working on a song that later became "The Singer Must Die." He taught me the melody and lyrics he'd written so far, though the lyrics were later augmented and changed in meaning and intention—like any authentic poet, Leonard was an endless reviser.

When I finally heard "A Singer Must Die" on his album *New Skin for the Old Ceremony* (released the following year, in 1974), I realized what he meant about working and re-working his compositions until he'd achieved the desired, exact, exquisite effect. The melody had evolved into a more intricate composition than the initial draft he'd played for me, and the lyrics now included some political/social commentary, where originally, they'd all dealt with a particular woman.

Another song on the album, which also seemed to reference that same woman, was called "Why Don't You Try." It was done in something of a honky-tonk style. I liked it so much that I composed another verse of my own:

Why don't you try a gainful occupation?
One that you'd be proud to tell the folks
I'm sure you'd great at entertaining for the soldiers
Or copyrighting ethnic Jewish jokes
Then you would know how it feels to earn a dollar
Then you would know what it's like to use your head
You could seduce the boss and then his little daughter
And be content with jewelry, jewelry instead

Another time, Leonard talked with me about his recently recorded song about Janis Joplin, "Chelsea Hotel #2" (also on *New Skin for the Old Ceremony*). He expressed some regret about having disclosed that it was about her.

"You know, Judy," he said, "I'm not one of those guys that likes to kiss and tell. And I'm not one who loses respect for a woman after I've had sex with her. I am grateful for every single woman who has granted me that privilege—the ones who like to fuck in phone booths [referring to a previous conversation where he'd experienced such a tryst] and the ones who don't. Deep down inside, I'm still little Lenny, the fifteen-year-old Jewish kid from Montreal who couldn't get a date to save his life. And the truth is: I still desire every single woman I meet."

And as far as I personally was concerned, Leonard was as good as his word. He never failed to respond to any communication I sent him, never failed to try and be helpful and supportive—which is all I'm willing to say about that subject.

In the summer of 1974, I actually spent one night at the Chelsea Hotel. I was with two friends/lovers, Patty and Karen, who worked as waitresses at a very upscale restaurant called The Deauville Inn, down the New Jersey shore, in Belmar. We'd arranged to get a day off together, and I drove us into Manhattan. We started out drinking at the famous White Horse Tavern, in the West Village, where Dylan Thomas was said to have drunk those fateful eighteen shots of whiskey that killed him (once he got back to his room in The Chelsea) and where Janis Joplin herself had hung out while in NYC.

Then we took a taxi to Max's Kansas City, the "in" place for the rock and roll crowd at that time. We scored a booth toward the front of the bar, and some of the regulars came over to chat with us—we were, after all, three very attractive young girls. One in the group, a young black guy with a beard, asked us if we'd like to try something more "stimulating," and we were just drunk enough to say, "Sure." I think what he gave us were black beauties or some other form of methedrine.

We stayed until closing. I was still coherent enough to let my companions know I wasn't fit to drive an hour and a half back to the Jersey shore. "Let's go over to the Chelsea Hotel and see if we can get a room," I suggested.

And so we agreed to continue our adventure and check out the Chelsea. We didn't have enough money for a cab (cabs in those days didn't accept credit cards) and Max's was in the East Village, not an easy walk to West 23rd Street. We flagged down a cab anyway and bargained with the young hippie-looking guy to take us there in exchange for a joint (also supplied by the guy from Max's). It was about 3:30 in the morning, and we really weren't sure we'd get a room for three, so one hid outside while the two of us went and asked politely if we could stay. I had one credit card at the time, and that's what we used to pay. The desk clerk was completely blasé about the whole thing. I guess they were pretty accustomed to late-night carousers showing up.

So, up we all went to the fourth floor. I doubt it was the same room Leonard had stayed in, but it seemed a reasonably shabby facsimile. Once I was in the double bed, I could sense that sex was on our collective minds but made no move to initiate it. I wasn't ready for a "Boy, was I drunk last night!" next-morning hangover. Since it was already almost four a.m., we just ended up going right to sleep.

Not long after, back at the Deauville Inn, the very refined mafioso maître d', whose name was Vincent, called Karen and me onto the wide stairs overlooking the main dining room. We were two of his very favorite waitresses. Pointing out a table in the middle of the floor, he asked us, "Want to see a couple of dykes?" He indicated two middle-aged women in short hair and leisure suits.

"How can you tell?" I asked him innocently.

"I can always tell," he answered, nodding.

"Ah," I said, "you can spot them a mile away, huh?"

"That's right," he nodded.

I don't know how Karen and I kept from bursting out laughing since we were already sleeping together by then!

And even there, in Belmar, New Jersey, Hydra found me. One of the other waitresses, who knew I had lived in Greece, brought a visiting friend, a young woman, over to meet me.

"Were you in Athens last summer, around a group house in Pangrati?" she asked me.

"Holy crow! How did you know that?" I asked incredulously.

"I was one of the people who came over one night to John and Rosemary's house and wished you a good journey and said goodbye." What a summer that was! But that's another story!

One of my favorite LC songs is entitled "One of Us Cannot Be Wrong." Ordinarily, I'd never dare to try to interpret Leonard's lyrics, but I'm pretty sure I know the derivation of that first verse:

I lit a thin green candle, to make you jealous of me
the room just filled up with mosquitos, they heard that my body was free*

Nothing really deep or mysterious about that one if you lived on Hydra in the early seventies, especially during the summer. Each house was plagued at night with mosquitos, largely because every house had a cistern built into the kitchen floor (a large underground receptacle for catching rainwater). And as there was no way to seal these structures, they were a natural breeding ground for mosquitos. Therefore, everyone would purchase mosquito coils (mosquito-repelling incense) from the local grocery store. These were thin, green coils attached to a metal clip

---

* "One of Us Cannot Be Wrong"—Leonard Cohen

on one end and lit from the other. One put them as close to the bed as one could and hoped the smoke they emitted would last all night.

Marianne told me something rather interesting about Leonard's original recording of that song; he did it in a studio in London, and at the end of the song, as with a lot of his vocals, he ends with "La la la la la lah la la lah la la lah," chanted over and over. Only this time (and it can easily be heard on the album *Songs of Love and Hate*), he got kind of carried away with the emotion in the song, and the chanting became a series of screams, louder and louder. Marianne said they had to go in and physically drag him out of the recording booth.

George told me about the reference in another one of Leonard's compositions, "The Master Song." George told me it was about a spiritual teacher and mystic named John Starr Cooke. Cooke was a student of Meher Baba and, while living in Algiers, became associated with a Sufi sect. While living in North Africa in the late fifties, he was bitten by some kind of very poisonous insect (or had some other mysteriously calamitous encounter) and was paralyzed for the rest of his life and was confined to a wheelchair. After that, Cooke returned to the United States and later settled in Tepozlan, Mexico. Marianne's first husband (who was always referred to as "Big Axel") became a student of Cooke's while traveling in North Africa, and one time, when Marianne and Leonard had a serious falling out, while she was living with him in Montreal, she fled to Mexico and stayed with Cooke.

She told me Leonard phoned there one day and asked her to return to Canada. "It wasn't very romantic," she said. He asked if she could also bring some "magic mushrooms" with her. And back she went. Anyway, that was who "The Master Song" was written about, or so George told me. There's a whole section about John Starr Cooke in Wikipedia—it is an interesting read.

As I mentioned, I'm a pretty good singer. I was in the church choir and glee club in high school, but none of that could have prepared me for singing alongside Leonard Cohen.

One day, after a couple of weeks of this, Leonard said to me, "You know, Judy, you sing as well as any backup singers I've worked with. If you like, I can introduce you to Clive Davis."

Singing was, in fact, something I wanted to do for a living. I'd dreamed of being a professional singer, but for some reason whether fear of success or fear of failure, that even today I can't fathom, I responded:

"Thank you, Leonard, but I feel I have to make it on my own."

How different my life and relationship with Leonard might have turned out had I said yes. It would have altered the dynamic of our friendship certainly.

Long ago, I wrote the following in my diary: "Regrets are the souvenirs of fools."

But if I have one huge, monumental regret, it's that I didn't take Leonard up on his offer.

I don't think it took long for Leonard to recognize that I was much more attracted to Marianne. I liked him, though, very much, and came to love him in the end. He was always very kind to me, and I knew him to be a generous, warm-hearted, compassionate man. He also had a wicked sense of humor and loved to play. One conversation we had at their kitchen table stands out in my mind because I was a bit of a player myself. Marianne was standing with her back to us at the sink, and Leonard looked up at me and said, "You know, Judy, Marianne doesn't really like you."

"That's how much you know, Leonard," I replied.

"No," he said. "I mean, she doesn't really like anyone."

"Well, no," I said, "because then she'd have to trust them, but she's crazy about me, Leonard."

With that, Marianne whirled around and put her arms around both of us. "You're both crazy," she said, "and I love you both!"

We laughed long and unreasonably hard. The moment passed.

But, oh—how well I remember.

Leonard always spent several hours each day working—writing in his studio. One day, he came out to the kitchen where Marianne and I were chatting. "I just thought of the most amazing title," he said. He seemed genuinely tickled. He placed a spiral notebook on the big oak kitchen table and actually climbed onto the table, crouching on his knees and elbows. "Listen to this," he announced dramatically, with great flourish and a long pause, "The Woman Being Born!" I think we both looked at him rather blankly.

We both repeated it dutifully, and then we said something like, "Wow, The Woman Being Born!" Honestly, I couldn't decide whether he was kidding us or if he was deadly serious. The Woman Being Born. It really left me puzzled and, to be honest, totally unenthused. His words, his way with words, and his poetic images and phrasing were what impressed me most in his music and poetry. But this phrase was just . . . too esoteric to be shared, I guess. He must have loved it, though, because I heard he used it as a working title for a book later renamed *My Life in Art.*

When Marianne first showed me Leonard's writing studio, she pointed out the front window, to the power line strung across the path, and told me that when electricity first appeared there, Leonard was not happy that modernity had arrived on Hydra. In fact, he was experiencing a bout of extreme depression and writer's block at the time.

"We'll have to find somewhere else to live now," he told her.

He much preferred the lights from oil lamps and candles. But as they were talking, a bird came and landed on the line.

"If a bird can get used to the wire, Leonard, you can get used to the wire," she said, referencing "Bird on the Wire" from 1969's *Songs From a Room*. "That's why I always felt closest to that song," she later confessed to me.

Marianne also told me about the derivation of a lyric in what would become Leonard's most famous and most covered song, "Hallelujah":

She tied you to a kitchen chair,
she broke your throne and she cut your hair*

It was in the context of a discussion we had about the difficulties Marianne had with their relationship. She told me Leonard just couldn't refuse any request made by a female. She said she thought it all originated in his rather complicated relationship with his mother. She was a very imposing and important person in his life. Marianne said that Leonard confessed to her that when he was a young child, his mother would insist on cutting his hair. When he got a little older and tried to refuse, she would use one of his father's neckties to *tie* him to a chair in their kitchen and snip away. Then she'd tell him that, like Sampson in the Bible, Leonard was completely in her power and would have to do anything she asked of him.

Marianne was pretty sure that was why he succumbed so easily to female imprecations. He just couldn't say no. And it was also why he sought to escape from relationships as often as he did. He just couldn't stay put. It was an example of the dilemma we all experience in love: constantly seeking a balance between acquiescence and resistance.

---

* "Hallelujah," Leonard Cohen

Another thing I learned from Marianne during that time was about Leonard's drug-taking. He has many times publicly admitted to doing a fair amount of drug experimentation in those days. It turned out, though, that one of the little-known reasons he settled on a Greek island was because Ritalin was available and legal as an over-the-counter drug there in the sixties. Leonard used it frequently to combat the depression that constantly plagued him back then. Marianne asked me if I had any Ritalin or if I knew where to get any as, by 1973, it was no longer available without a prescription. Leonard wanted to find out if any of the younger foreign residents or travelers had any. But, of course, he didn't want anyone to know he was looking for some. I told her I'd ask around but offhand didn't know of any way to get it. She thanked me, and I promised to mention neither her nor Leonard in my inquiries. I never could find any for him, though, and during that time, I never saw him take anything stronger than beer or wine.

One day when I was hanging out with Marianne in the kitchen, Leonard came out from his study to get a drink and saw Marianne clutching her abdomen. He asked what was wrong. She said she had a stabbing pain in her stomach and didn't know why. He said, "Let's try something."

He sat down on the floor in front of the kitchen table with his back against the wall and his legs crossed in an Indian style. He told Marianne to sit facing him in the same posture. Then he said, "Point to your pain in my body."

She leaned over and touched him in the middle of his stomach.

"Good," he said, then repeated, "Now point to your pain in my body."

She did it again, and the sequence went on like that for about five minutes, with her pointing to her pain on his stomach and he acknowledging and repeating the instruction.

Finally, when he repeated his instruction for maybe the twentieth time, she hesitated for a minute and said, "It's moved."

"Good," he replied very calmly. "Now point to your pain in my body."

She was quiet for a few seconds, then looked up.

"It's gone," she said.

He smiled and again acknowledged, "Good."

Then he got up and went back to work.

It was sometime later that I found out he was using a "clearing process" he'd learned while studying Scientology. You have to figure there is something in it that attracts people. So, I guess if one can "heal" someone by giving them your undivided attention and focusing energy on a physical problem, it can't be all bad. For me, though, witnessing this was yet another instance of how much Marianne and Leonard had allowed me into the little, perhaps just-dying ember, of their time together. But it was their little family just the same.

It was now the heart of a sizzling Greek summer heatwave, so while we were in the house, Marianne and I usually just wore bikini underwear and went topless while Leonard wore khaki army-style shorts and no shirt. There was no erotic or exhibitionist element in it. It was just too hot for clothes—necessary nudity, one might say.

Another time, Marianne and I were up in their bedroom where there was a bit more of a breeze, talking and laughing, and she was literally telling me the story of her life when Leonard appeared in the doorway. He took hold of the door jamb above his head and leaned in, just kind of watching us. "Do you need something, Leonard?" Marianne asked. He just smiled and shook his head. Then he turned and went back to his studio. "I think he's a bit jealous," Marianne told me. "He's used to being the center of attention, especially from young girls."

"Well," I said, "don't you think he gets enough of that?"

"Oh yes," she replied. "More than enough!"

One day, Leonard was going down to the Four Corners shop and shouted up to Marianne and me in the upstairs bedroom, asking if we needed anything. Marianne leaned out the window to where he waited on the steps below. As she listed a few things she needed for dinner, I started kissing her on her bare back. Leonard couldn't see me. As he left, Marianne turned and hugged me, saying, "You really are just as crazy as the rest of us, aren't you?" More laughing then. We did much laughing in those days. But Marianne still had her mood swings and remained exquisitely elusive in endless ways.

One night, she and I went down to the port and had a beer at Tasso's, as per usual (Leonard rarely left the house and was not at all into casual socializing). Marianne started chatting with two young Greek guys at the next table. To my consternation, she invited them to accompany us to Cavos, the discotheque. *What the hell is she up to now?* I wondered. I knew she had absolutely no interest in these guys and was just being typically provocative. As we walked toward the stairs that led up to the disco, I told her in exasperation, "You go ahead, I'm going to go for a walk."

I walked alone to the edge of the harbor road and sat down around the bend by the cannons. Sure enough, after about five minutes, she reappeared.

"Why do you do that, Marianne?" I asked. "Why do you always try to provoke me?"

"I don't know," she replied. "It just scares me sometimes. If we had met up in some strange city and had a brief affair that would be one thing. But it's like you've become a part of the family. You fit in so well . . . with Axel . . . with Leonard. It's not just about me."

"I know," I said. "It scares me too."

So off we went back to Cavos. And after hours of dancing and drinking, sometimes together, sometimes me with one partner, she with another, she suddenly whirled around toward me, looked me in the eye and put her finger on my lips, then very quickly drew it down the front of my body in a line until it ended at my crotch.

Then she turned and danced away.

Well, Kiddo, I told myself, *you are really a goner now!*

Many years later, when I was once again involved in a difficult and complicated romantic affair, a good friend made a really excellent observation: "Just about the time you tell yourself, 'I'd better get out of this situation before it's too late' . . . it's too late!"

Marianne told me almost everything about her past romantic life. I found out I was not the first female she'd been involved with. She told me herself about at least three others, including the well-known Native American folk singer Julie Felix, that she'd had affairs with.

Leonard even wrote a poem about it. It appears on page 47 in *The Energy of Slaves* and is untitled:

> What character could possibly engage my boredom, that
> exquisite spoiled princess in the palace of my failure? She
> refuses even to imagine him with whom I must inspire her
> hopefulness, and she barely speaks to me.
> The story is already complicated by my indifference.
> I believe she longs for a woman.
> She does not want the gift to come from me.
> She wants to wear delicate men's trousers and live with this woman
> in a port town where they will perfect sweet rituals
> such as walking together at twilight smoking cigarillos past
> shadowy retired fishermen who learn to accept them as
> another species of bird which they would judge no more

fiercely than the seagull or the heron.
I could have created such a woman out of the one or two
women who loved me, but in those days, I had no taste for
monsters, although I must admit they did.

Another evening, we went together to a party at Alexis' house
(more on Alexis later). I wasn't noticing how much Marianne was
drinking, but at one point, she just collapsed on the floor in a heap. No
one could get her to stand up or move. I tried, but it was to no avail.
She wasn't passed out or anything, just refusing to move. People kept
on dancing around her. Finally, I went off with some others, down to
the harbor for coffee.

I must have stayed out all night, which wasn't unusual for me in
those days. I kept waiting for her to show up again, but she never did.
So finally, around six a.m., I left Tasso's café and climbed the hill toward
home. When I got to the turn in the path toward Marianne's house, I
thought I'd check to make sure she got back okay.

The door to the inside staircase, actually one half of a double door,
was open. That was always the signal that visitors were welcome. If that
door was closed, you didn't bother knocking. I was a little surprised that
it was open so early, but I entered, climbed the stairs, and turned right
in the hallway that led to the kitchen. Leonard was sitting at the table.

"Marianne isn't here, Judy," he said.

Ah, that's why the door was open so early. I remember feeling
shocked.

"You're kidding," I said. "Where is she then?"

"I don't know, but I don't think she's alone," he replied.

Then he said something that really surprised me: "Sex with Marianne was always excruciating, but I desired her very much."

It's that way with most of us, I thought. We always want the ones we
can't completely possess.

I sat down then, at my usual place at the table, and only a few minutes later, Marianne walked in. She looked as surprised to see us both there as I'd been in not finding her at home.

"Let me make you breakfast," she said.

And so she did, and nothing more was spoken about it.

Leonard also told me, possibly that same morning, that there were "two very different Mariannes": a loving, considerate, maternal, sober one and an unpredictable, impulsive—even a little bit crazy—one when drunk. I had no problem believing him. I'd unquestionably witnessed both.

I do remember another conversation I had with Leonard about Marianne, where he told me that although he had lived with Marianne several different places—Montreal and New York, most prominently—the only place he really experienced her as a muse was on Hydra.

"I don't think I ever wrote a song that was inspired by her, unless we were here together on Hydra," he said. "Here it just seemed to be a natural extension of the place itself. Anywhere else, even when she tried to encourage me, or inspire me, it didn't work."

One evening, when Marianne was in Athens, a group of us all went out to dinner at Douskos, as we often did. George came, along with Anthony Kingsmill and several others. Aside from George, Anthony was one of Leonard's oldest and closest friends on Hydra. I don't recall how I first got to know him myself, but he was ubiquitous on the island. He'd been there for a long time and was very well respected. At the time, he was about forty-seven, had a young American wife, Christina, from Chicago, and a two-year-old daughter, Emily.

Anthony was an artist, and he was a very talented one. I believe he was considered to be the best of the Hydra artist group. But he was also a very, very serious alcoholic (and not a terribly good husband or father, as well). He was one of the most intelligent, droll, and erudite people

I've ever known and, just like my joy in being accepted into Leonard's and Marianne's "family," I was equally delighted to be considered a friend to Anthony.

And it was all because of a song.

I can't remember the first time he found out I knew both verses to "Danny Boy" and asked me to sing it for him. I don't think I was ever after in his presence and not required to sing him that song. And every time I did, he wept. Which is just the sort of reaction one wants when singing that timeless classic.

Anthony was a very imposing and impressive personage with a razor-sharp mind, a cutting wit, and a wicked sense of humor. If he liked you, he was the nicest, kindest, most tolerant, and supportive friend. But if he didn't like you, look out—especially if you annoyed him when he'd been drinking. Which was most of the time.

On another night, we all went out to dinner together. Leonard and Anthony and I were the last to leave (and, yes, I had sung "Danny Boy"). The other Irish revolutionary song that both Leonard and Anthony loved was "Kevin Barry," a heartbreaking ballad about the eighteen-year-old Irish lad who helped to start the Easter Rebellion of 1918 by blowing up the Dublin Post Office building (actually, I later looked Kevin Barry up in Wikipedia, and although he was involved in attacking a truckload of English soldiers—two of whom were killed—he was not involved in the famous post office attack where the British troops were garrisoned). Barry was hanged immediately after his capture and remained a hero to some Irish people.

Ever the naïf at the time, I actually thought I was introducing them to that song for the first time. Much later, I found out Leonard had been familiar with it for many years and had even included it at times in his repertoire . . . but he was far too kind to tell me that. After "Danny Boy," I was usually commanded to sing "Kevin Barry."

We ended up at Tasso's late in the evening. Anthony and Leonard told me something about Anthony's background that I think very few people knew: Anthony, the apparently quintessential Brit, was actually born in Eastern Europe—Poland or Czechoslovakia, I think they said. And they claimed to be long-lost cousins as well, because Anthony's original last name, before his British stepfather adopted him, was a form of Cohen. I seem to remember hearing something about his mother escaping just before World War II and immigrating to England because she was Jewish, and so was Anthony. I don't think they were leading me on—though the cousin bit was undoubtedly an exaggeration. I looked up Anthony's stepfather and found out he was a British writer, Hugh Kingsmill, well-known for his pointed wit (probably where his stepson got it).

At about three a.m., the port was fairly deserted, and we ended up at Leonard's house. I was pretty drunk by then and soon crawled onto the Russian bed in the little downstairs bedroom and passed out. About an hour later, Anthony and Leonard came into the room and tried to rouse me.

"Sing 'Danny Boy' again, Judy. Come on, one more time," they both entreated.

I just shook my head and turned over.

"You're both nuts," I told them, and I went back to sleep.

George gave another party not long after Leonard arrived. A whole bunch of people was invited—newbies on the island for the first time as well as the entire ex-pat crowd. George asked Leonard if he'd come by, too. As I've mentioned, Leonard was not very sociable, especially in large crowds, but he said okay since George was one of his oldest friends.

There was a young guy wearing a top hat who came with a guitar. He was just someone George and I had started chatting with in the port.

He'd come to Hydra, he told us, because he was such a big fan of Leonard Cohen. The party took over George's whole house, and a big crowd of people, including Mr. Top Hat, was up on the second floor, out on the terrace. Leonard stayed below on the first floor, near the kitchen, dancing by himself to music that was playing.

I went up to look for the young fan. When I found him, I said, "Hey, Leonard Cohen is downstairs."

"Oh, sure. Right," he said. "You know it's not nice to tease someone like that."

It took me a long time to convince him that I wasn't joking. But when he finally went downstairs to see for himself, Leonard—as if he'd intuited the intrusion—had just left.

Given Leonard's inclination toward solitude, I felt particularly lucky and particularly blessed to be so welcomed into his house and family. Another time, I think it was after Marianne had decamped to Athens again, I was sitting on Leonard's terrace with our friend Felicity, chatting with him.

"How many great loves do you think a person has in their life?" Leonard asked us.

We thought about that for a few seconds, then I answered, "Just one."

Felicity thought about it for a minute and then opined, "I think it's probably two: one when you're young, a first love if you will, and another when you're older, a more mature love."

Leonard looked at both of us, then shook his head in my direction and nodded. "Just one," he said, somewhat wistfully.

I've since read a couple of Leonard Cohen biographies, and one of the things I was always puzzled about was how they characterized the separation between Leonard's relationship with Marianne and the later one with Suzanne. In my opinion, after being there for that time, there was quite an overlap. After all, Adam, his son, was almost two years old in 1973, and yet, Leonard still considered a part of his life to be with Marianne and Axel on Hydra. And I also knew this to be true: Leonard and Marianne still slept in the same bed, in the same room, where they always had. But that summer, the summer of 1973, would be the last time they were ever together in the same house at the same time.

One day, when we were sitting on the terrace drinking beer and chatting, he said to me, "You know, Judy, I don't really know anymore where I belong. When I'm here with Marianne and Axel, I feel like this is my home, this is my life. But when I'm in Montreal with Suzanne and the baby, I feel that's where my life is."

In what, in retrospect, can only be described as youthful hubris, I intoned: "That's what makes Hydra so special, isn't it Leonard? Here, George is not really so Greek anymore, I'm not American, and you're not Jewish. We're all just living on Hydra."

He shook his head at that rather presumptuous remark. "Oh no, Judy," he said gently. "I'm really a Jew, always a Jew."

Not long afterward, he wrote this poem:

> Anyone who says I'm not a Jew
> is not a Jew★

He also told me, during that conversation, how he divided his homes in his mind:

"The house in Montreal will always be for Suzanne and the baby," he said, "but this house is for Marianne."

Suzanne Elrod was the mother of Leonard's son, Adam, born in 1971, and later of his daughter, Lorca, born in 1975. Suzanne was not

---

★ "Not a Jew," Leonard Cohen

the subject of his iconic song—that was a different Suzanne (Suzanne Verdal, the former wife of Québécois sculptor Armand J. R. Vaillancourt). Leonard's arrangement struck me as fair since Marianne had sold her house up Kalo Pigadi—the one she'd purchased with her former husband, Axel Jensen, which he'd left for her and little Axel—to help support herself and Leonard in their first years together. But thanks to Suzanne's jealousy and desire to wipe Marianne from his life, even that was not to be.

One of the main things that attracted artists to Greece was the light. It's actually known as "Greek Light"; very pure and unfiltered, it allows a painter to easily duplicate what's in front of him (or her). Hydra was supposed to have the very best Greek Light because there were no exhaust fumes or gasoline engines to speak of. Most automated things like refrigerators were run by electricity or propane. Aside from its beauty, that's one of the major reasons so many painters flock there.

Like Paris in the in the thirties, Harlem in the forties, Greenwich Village in the fifties, and San Francisco in the sixties, Hydra in the seventies was experiencing its Golden Age. I met so many talented and amazing people during that first summer on Hydra: artists, writers, singer/songwriters, poets, and so on. It was really an incredible fraternity of friends and lovers. And over the years, there were feuds and favorites, and sometimes, they would trade places, but in the end, we were all a sort of big, creative, rambunctious family. And each of the persons who occupied my time there and ended up in my journal entries was either close friends (and sometimes more) with Marianne and/or Leonard. We all belonged to the same *parea* (Greek for a group of friends who regularly gather together to share their experiences about life).

When I first met Alexis Bolens on the rocks in Kamini, he was a tall, handsome, impressive, barrel-chested man who carried himself with rakish dignity. He was a ladies' man, no doubt. And he lived in a house up Kalo Pigadi that I found out much later was the same one originally owned by Marianne and her first husband, Axel Jensen. The house clung to the side of the mountain a good way up from the main road, and Alexis had done much work on it, extending it halfway around the hill. It had one of the few swimming pools at that time, embedded into the hill, and a cool bathroom built into the walls of the rocks like a cave.

While sitting on the swimming rocks, we'd all chat about our lives, aspirations, big plans for the future, and so on, but one of Alexis' favorite pastimes was telling jokes. So I told him one of mine in return:

An itinerant miner came into the only saloon in a frontier town and asked, "Are there any women in this town?"

"No," the bartender replied, "but the guys around here use the wild pig herd at the outskirts of town."

"Oh, no," the miner retorted. "I'm not into that."

After getting some supplies, off he went, back into the hinterland. Six months later, he returned. "Any women yet?" He asked, hopefully.

"No," the bartender said, shaking his head sadly. "But there is still the herd of wild pigs. . . ."

Sighing, the miner said, "Forget it," and off he went to prospect some more.

Six months passed, and once again, he showed up in the saloon, but this time, he asked, "Okay, where are the wild pigs?"

The bartender gave him specific directions, and after surveying the herd, the miner picked out what looked like a young, not-too-hairy female. He brought her back to the saloon, took her up to his room, gave her a bath, and put a big pink ribbon on her.

Actually, now she didn't look half bad.

He carried her back down and placed her on a barstool. Immediately, the bartender ducked, and all the other patrons ran screaming out into the street. The miner was completely baffled. When the bartender peeked just above the edge of the bar, the miner said, "I thought you told me all the guys used the wild pigs!"

"Yes," replied the bartender, "but that's Black Bart's girl!"

We all ate at Douskos almost every night. One evening, it was just George, Leonard, and me. (Marianne was in Athens yet again.) The taverna was very popular with the yachting crowd as well as the foreign ex-pats. A large table of Scandinavians kept staring at us as we ate. Leonard seemed pretty unfazed, but I knew they'd all recognized him, and I felt very proud to be having dinner with him.

While Marianne was away, a young Jewish girl from Montreal named Hazel arrived. I first encountered her sitting on the floor in Marianne's kitchen. She knew them both from their time in that city and was especially close to Leonard. In fact, as of this writing, she still lives in one-third of a triplex he owns in Montreal. Speaking about her at the time, Leonard told me something I was skeptical about. He said, motioning toward the kitchen where she was still sitting, "That girl put me through more changes in one week than Marianne has in all these years." *Yeah right*, Leonard, I thought, but I said nothing.

I tried to leave Hydra several times during that period. Leonard offered to give me some money if I wanted to stay on. Besides being incredibly honest, open, and—at thirty-eight—strikingly attractive, that's how kind and generous he was.

"I have money, Judy," he said. "I can give you some if you really want to stay here."

But Marianne had made it very clear in several of our talks that she felt people took advantage of Leonard's generosity, especially young women, and I didn't want him to think I was one of those.

So, I said, "I can't take your money Leonard, but thank you for the offer."

One day, walking down Donkey Shit Lane with my knapsack, when I thought I was departing, I ran into Rick Vick, the boyfriend of our artist friend, Jane. "Leaving again are you, Judy?" he asked.

"Yes, going to Paris."

"Right. Well, see you tomorrow then," he joked. And though I don't remember what prevented me that time, the next day did find me still on Hydra.

Later that summer, during my first sojourn on Hydra, as it became pretty clear to me that while Leonard was there at the house, it was very unlikely anything physical was going to happen between Marianne and me, and I was getting very short on cash, I once again made plans to make my departure.

Two days before my departure date, another houseguest, Gil Simmons, had arrived at George's. He was an heir to the Simmons mattress fortune, and we first met when he took an apartment in Athens and got hooked up with the ex-pat community. Of course, his flat was located in Kolonaki, the most expensive area of the city. Marianne and I had gone over to see it while we were in town together. It wasn't palatial or anything, but it was a really pleasant, bright, open space with a fabulous view over Athens from a broad terrace facing the city.

Like many Americans planning on an extended stay in Athens, he was rumored to be working for the CIA. Anyway, as I was making plans for departure (yet again), Gil showed up at George's house. He was on an "island-hopping" jaunt to Hydra and other destinations. He stayed a couple of days. In the meantime, George said his goodbyes to me and went on his own into Athens on business. I saw Marianne the following day and told her that George was away and Gil was leaving the next morning. "I'll have the house all to myself for at least one night," I said.

She nodded. "Good," she whispered.

So, off Gil went, on the morning boat, to see another not-nearly-so-picturesque-nor-interesting island. Spetsi was the Saronic Gulf Island where there had once been a boys' school run by a private British organization. The novelist John Fowles had taught there just before World War II and used it as the locale for *The Magus*, his terrific book set in Greece. But apart from that claim to fame, Spetsi was quite provincial and boring.

Left all alone in the big house on the hill, I went down to the port and sat at Tasso's all day to say my farewells to what had, by now, become a burgeoning foreign population. After several drinks, kisses, and promises to "keep in touch," I went up the hill to have a final dinner with Leonard and Marianne.

Marianne cooked for us and, as was pretty typical, the meal went on quite late. I thought for sure that she and I had an unspoken agreement to spend the night together up at George's house where he had a large, elevated, wooden sea-captain's bed that you reached via a built-in staircase. But then we heard footsteps on the outside stairs, and Gil Simmons walked in through the kitchen doorway.

I don't think I've ever been more shocked and less delighted to see anybody.

"Hi folks," he said. "You were right. Spetsi is completely boring— I caught the last boat back!"

Later, when Marianne and I were alone in the kitchen cleaning up, she looked at me with real regret and said, "I thought we'd finally have one last opportunity to spend time together in George's big, beautiful captain's bed."

"Yeah," I sighed. "I kind of had the same thought myself."

Oh, the vicissitudes of life.

So I ended up staying at Leonard and Marianne's that night, and Leonard did one of the most generous and unselfish things for me.

When it was time to turn in, he said, "It's such a pretty night and still so hot inside, I'm going to sleep here on the terrace on the Russian sofa." That left the bedroom available for Marianne and me.

Once in bed, I tried to kiss her, but she shook her head no.

"I can't while he is in the house," she told me.

Damn—this was just never going to happen, I thought. I reluctantly moved over to the other side of the bed.

Then she said, "Well, you don't have to sleep so far away."

Back I went to her side. With a hug, a kiss, and a chaste embrace, we both fell asleep.

Marianne accompanied me to the afternoon ferry the next day. As we sat in a quayside café waiting for the boat, she stared out into the harbor and said softly, "Well, I guess you know I love you."

Very few things in my life have ever touched me as much as this simple confession.

I nodded and responded, "I guess you know I love you too."

She smiled more broadly then, shook her head, and looked at me. "Oh, yes," she said. "I know that."

I boarded the boat and waved goodbye. A Tony Bennett song, of all things, began to run through my mind. But it wasn't San Francisco that I left my heart in—it was back there, receding from me, on Hydra.

I flew to Paris the next day after spending the night with John Zervos and Rosemary Donnelly in Athens. In Paris, I stayed with the brother of my college friend Mary-Luc, Jean, who was an ethnic Chinese man from Vietnam, and his wife. They lived in the southern suburb of Bagneaux. But Hydra was not far from my thoughts, and it was not finished with me yet—not by a long shot.

Several days after arriving in France, I accompanied their neighbor, Doctor Armand, to the Greek travel office to pick up some brochures and information as he and his family were planning a driving trip to Greece the following month. After we got everything he wanted, we stopped at a little bistro for dinner.

They seated us, as was customary when places were crowded, at a four-top table already occupied by two French men. Armand spread the brochures out between us, and we talked some more about what he should see on his trip.

One of our French table companions pointed to the flyers and asked in English, "You like Greece?"

"Yes," I responded. "I just returned from there."

"Where do you stay in Greece?" he asked.

"On one of the islands."

"Which island?" he persisted.

"Hydra," I replied.

"I know Hydra," he said, nodding, then: "Do you know Marianne?"

Oh Jeez! I thought, *where the hell did that come from?!*

"Who are you?!" I demanded.

"I'm Jean Marc."

Jean Marc! Marianne had shown me his picture only the week before. He'd been her lover for several years. He even followed her to New York, where she was living with Little Axel in Leonard's loft on Stanton Street in Lower Manhattan while Leonard stayed mostly at the Chelsea Hotel with his new rock and roll buddies. Jean Marc was wild about her. He was a kindred soul. Of course, I didn't let on about my feelings for Marianne, only saying I thought she was wonderful, and we'd spent a lot of time together.

I don't remember how it all transpired, but I do know that I spent the next week being a surrogate lover to Jean Marc. The day after we met, I joined him and his friend from our table, who happened to be the French Minister of Culture, at the minister's office. Back in those days, there were no cell phones, of course, but the minister had an international WATS (Wide Area Telephone Service) line. We arranged to make a call to Marianne via George Lialios' phone.

When she answered, I told her I was calling with a friend of hers in Paris. Then Jean Marc got on the line.

Lots and lots of surprising, sometimes astonishing, things have happened to me in connection to Hydra. But I'm pretty sure that for Marianne, this was utterly dumbfounding as well. In a city of four million people, one week after leaving her on Hydra, I had randomly encountered one of her most cherished and fervent lovers in Paris.

I spent the next week with Jean Marc at his little apartment, though at some point, I must have gone down to Bagneau to get my belongings from Jean and his wife. Jean Marc was charming, very good-looking, and extremely generous, but he was also a first-class male chauvinist. We spent time with his friend, the minister, and any time the three of us were together, they spoke in French to one another, although both were extremely fluent in English. In fact, the minister had actually taught for a time at Marquette University in the United States. To add insult to injury, any time we met with another English speaker, if he was male, they would converse in English.

I felt like a very indulged pet. Get her a beer or a glass of wine, find her a comfy chair—then completely ignore her. That got old really fast. But after a week, Jean Marc decided to go to Greece, and I decided to head to a friend's place in Cambridge. Jean Marc magnanimously bought the student charter ticket for me.

Once in Cambridge, I enjoyed seeing my British friends again and hanging out at the Fort Saint George, one of the oldest pubs in England, right on the River Cam and, as luck would have it, our local. But all I really wanted was to get back to Hydra. I was missing it and Marianne terribly. So I wrote to her and mentioned the possibility of returning. She wrote me back right away. It was just a postcard, but it said something like, "Seeing Leonard and me here and now, it would be good if you returned, so yes, do come back." I didn't realize, at that point, that Jean Marc had delayed his trip to Greece and was not there yet. I was still low on funds, so I wrote to my two best friends in LA who knew how much I had loved the city of Edinburgh when I'd visited Scotland. To each of them, I wrote the same thing:

"In Edinburgh. I'm healthy as hell, but on Hydra, I'm a star! Please lend me $75.00 so I can go back there."

And they did. The round-trip fare was $150.00, and as soon as I got the money, I booked a ticket at the student travel office in Cambridge. I was once again a world traveler heading for adventure.

Three weeks later, I climbed Donkey Shit Lane and rapped on George's door. I hadn't had time to contact him, so he wasn't expecting me. When he answered my knock, I said, "Hi, George, is it okay?" Smiling, he swung the door wider and said, "Yes, of course!"

Just as I'd hoped, I was welcomed back. It felt so good, like coming home. George led me to one of the mid-level bedrooms as he was now having my old room painted. This one was bigger, with a double bed and two windows overlooking the back garden—no fireplace, though, and not as much charm. What did I care about charm?

After putting my stuff away, I joined George for a glass of wine. "How is everyone?" I asked. "How's Leonard? How's Marianne?" It turned out that a ton of things could change in three weeks' time. "Leonard has gone back to Montreal," George told me. "He left a little after you did. Jean Marc is staying with Marianne now."

Well, that was not what I'd hoped to hear. I knew Jean Marc was heading for Hydra, but he'd said he was only staying a brief time. I'd assumed that he'd have come and gone by now. This was going to make things a little more interesting—and not in a good way. The best-laid plans . . . Platitudes notwithstanding, things didn't go as I'd hoped in my reunion with Marianne. I saw them at Tasso's the next morning.

"Hi, I'm back," I announced, approaching their table.

Marianne got up and hugged me, but when I looked at Jean Marc, he simply said: "You bitch."

"Ah," I replied. "You read the letter."

"You bitch," he repeated.

Oh, yeah, I might just have mentioned in my letter to Marianne that I thought Jean Marc was a terrible chauvinist who'd treated me more like a puppy than a girlfriend or even a date (or even a human being). I sat down and joined them anyway. He didn't really seem *that* upset. After all, he was back with the great love of his life, so he could afford to be genial. But, no more open-door welcomes, no more dinners, no more long talks and exchanged secrets and laughs with Marianne.

I did still spend time with her son Axel and the rest of the summer colony. Another Hydra ex-pat, Dimitri Gassoumis, a Greek American from San Francisco, whose mother was from Hydra, had rented a house further up on the island next to the new cathedral. Dimitri was an artist, too, and a very talented one. Much later, Monika and I bought his painting of the Hydra harbor from the vantage point of one of the swimming areas off the coast. It still hangs in our living room.

Anyway, one evening in 1973, we were all invited to a party at Dimitri's. It was the age of sex, drugs, and rock and roll, and I'd bought some windowpane acid while passing through London. I'd dropped LSD before in a more peaceful, controlled setting, but for some reason, George, Vicki Zevgolis (a Greek American from Virginia, who often vacationed on Hydra, staying with Alexis Bolens at his house), and I decided to take it that night.

The party was large, and there were many summer people there whom I didn't know. Helga (George's friend—the footsie-playing one) had returned to stay with him and had brought her fourteen-year-old son Michel with her. While George and I sat on the terrace, tripping and quite transfixed with the view, she came up to us indignantly complaining that some of the guys at the party were sharing their hash with Michel.

"Isn't that awful?" she exclaimed. "What can I do?"

I don't know how I managed to contain my laughter. If she'd only known the condition we were in—the friends she'd turned to for help! We tried to be sympathetic, but she could see she wasn't getting any assistance from us and went off to deal with it on her own.

Such parties were not uncommon. Here's a journal entry from that time:

Sometimes it feels good to me, and not incongruous at all, to be able to listen to Janis Joplin and John Prine and Leonard on a really good stereo system (which George's house has). In our last days at the house, we have been eating some incredible meals. The four of us take turns buying and preparing our own specialties. Last night, we had chili with cornbread and a big salad and beer and, for dessert, fresh fruit salad of peaches and grapes and apples and oranges with cognac poured over the top and vanilla ice cream on top of that.

The night before, we had invited some French artists over for dinner. They brought some hash with them, and we all got very stoned. Ironically, Christian, who is probably one of the most serious and humorless people I've ever met, lives off an income he acquired compiling a joke book (!) entitled COLLECTION DES HISTOIRES DROLLES. The others who came were his eighteen-year-old niece who is half Tahitian; his friend Bernard, who is tall and thin and quite attractive and wears lovely silver

jewelry; Jean Noel, who is almost too pretty and is aligned with Bernard;
and lastly, Guy, whom I guess fits not quite as well in the same category.
The evening was filled with many ebbs and flows and interesting undercur-
rents, and I decided not to join all of them for a midnight swim.

The meal, however, was magnificent! Coq au vin flambéed in brandy,
string beans cooked with nutmeg, salad with the kind of delicious dressing
only George can make (with first-pressed olive oil from his family's com-
pany in Patras), spiced rice in chicken broth, vodka and grapefruit juice, red
wine, and homemade peach pie with ice cream. It gives the kind of pleasure
I refuse to feel guilty about. A sense of integrity does not require a Spartan
existence— not even in Greece!

I later came to regret the fact that, in those days, age, sex, and
nationality didn't seem to matter. Anything went for anyone interested.
It didn't work out so well for some of the younger ones. Michel became
a heroin addict (after a serious motorcycle accident back in Paris) and
later died of an overdose. And many other young people there did not
fare much better. I regretfully concluded that the big kids should never
be permitted to play with the little kids. But back then, we naively didn't
think there was anything wrong with it.

The remainder of the summer passed. I went with friends to swim
almost every day. There was a certain set of rocks halfway between the
main town of Hydra and the village of Kamini, which was normally only
utilized by local ex-pats, especially the ones from Montreal. In fact, we
called it "Montreal Beach." This was where I'd gone swimming that
fateful day I first met George Lialios and changed the direction of my
life. It was tricky to get to these rocks because one had to climb down
a long granite staircase with no handrail, carved into the cliffs, and then
jump from one narrow rock to another before the path widened into

a flatter area where we all hung out. All summer long, everyone who knew about the place (and there weren't many) had staked out their own spot on a certain rock or two where we would lay out towels to sunbathe and swim.

One of the regulars was Naná, a Greek woman who lived in New York City but owned a house on Hydra where she spent each August. She was a friend of Leonard's, too. Naná always came at the same time to the same rock. One day, a French tourist nobody knew somehow discovered our little enclave, climbed down, and laid his towel out on Naná's habitual spot. When she arrived shortly after, she tapped him imperiously on the shoulder and said, "That's my rock. You're in my place."

Being French and every bit as inclined to rudeness as a Greek, he replied, "How is it your rock? I don't see your name on it!" He then turned over and resumed sunbathing.

Well, that didn't sit very well with Naná. She left in a huff. But the next day when we arrived to swim, we found that she'd gone to the local hardware store and there, on her rock in black spray paint, it now read:

NANÁ'S ROCK!

One thing Leonard liked to do—well, we all did, actually—was go swimming in the nude. Now, that was rather tricky on Hydra. We'd go very early in the day, after the fishermen had gone out to sea but before they brought back their catch mid-morning. It was so incredibly beautiful to swim in that gorgeous, pure, azure Aegean with nothing on and the water caressing one's bare body. The good news for us was the fishing boats, called *caiques*, were very noisy, so when we heard them approaching around the bend, we all exited the water and quickly covered up. Of course, we always brought towels and bathing suits with us because those cranky Albanian Greeks did not approve of nudity. If one got caught, they'd be arrested and likely kicked off the island after paying a pretty hefty fine. In fact, if they even saw a woman bathing *topless*, she could be in big trouble. Although there were many nude beaches in Greece at the time—on Corfu, on Crete, and especially on Mykonos—one didn't get away with that around the very conservative Greeks on Hydra.

I still saw Marianne and Jean Marc in the port quite often and joined them for a beer and a chat when I did. One time, I vividly remember sitting opposite Marianne in the big rattan chairs at Tasso's and she casually put her bare foot up on the edge of my chair next to my bare leg. Again, it was done with no visible reaction from any of us, yet I knew, without a doubt, that all three of us were more focused on that foot and its location than on our conversation.

Another day when we were all sitting there, Jean Marc actually had an inkling of intuition. Watching Marianne and me talking, seeing our level of intensity, maybe even emotional connection, he blurted out, "Were you two lovers?!"

Marianne looked straight at me and shook her head.

"No, no, we were only both *your* lovers," she said.

Although true, I knew that it was something she wasn't very happy about. He still looked suspicious but seemed mollified. There are none so blind as those who will not see.

At another point, I asked Marianne, "Why did you write and tell me to come back?"

"Leonard was still here. Jean Marc hadn't arrived. When he did, he gave me $300 and I didn't know when or even if you were really returning. What would you have me do?"

Now, I'm not totally naïve when it comes to certain incandescent personalities and their interest in and genuine connection to their admirers. And I know all about saying what you think someone wants to hear. Still, it gave me a little—if cold—comfort.

I remember having a conversation with our friend Felicity around that time.

"You almost seem to be enjoying your heartbreak and the drama it causes you," she observed.

"In a way, I do," I said. "It somehow makes me feel more alive."

In all honesty, Marianne was not the first woman I'd been involved with emotionally. In fact, one of the motivations for this long sojourn I was on in Europe was to escape another frustrating but very, very compelling (obsessive, actually) relationship I had endured for the previous three years while finishing my undergrad degree at California State University at Northridge in the San Fernando Valley.

When Leonard had asked us, "How many great loves does one have in life?" this person, this beautiful girl named Rita, two years my junior, who was also a graduate student in the philosophy department, immediately came to mind. She was, in fact, the great love of my life. And whoever it was that claimed unrequited love was the strongest kind, well, they knew what they were talking about.

It wasn't that Marianne reminded me of Rita, although they were both intelligent, funny, engaging, and had a distinctive, very striking physicality. It was more that they both had the same irresistible attractiveness to anyone to whom they chose to grant attention. "Incandescent Personalities," I call them, and they seemed to be my downfall.

I was aware enough to know that if one were still resisting the identity of being gay (a term that was only just then coming into general usage)—and I was certainly resisting due to my "good Catholic girl" background—then being involved with another woman who was essentially straight but chose me to be the exception, confirmed my feelings of specialness. It made my own sexuality seem more ambiguous and, in a way, safer. We weren't gay after all, certainly weren't *lesbians* (God, no!). We were just "different" in a "very secret, special way."

It was such a common phenomenon in all-girl college dormitories, they even had an acronym for it: LUG. Lesbian Until Graduation.

I could write a book about those three years of being involved with Rita with whom I also never slept—well, sexually speaking, at least. I actually used to share a bed with her every night in the early months of our association. Late one evening, when she was leaving my apartment (which I shared with two roommates), she asked, "Are you coming?"

As we approached the door, I said, "Don't you think it's kind of weird for me to leave my place and follow you home just to go to sleep?"

She replied with a laugh, "I think everything about this is kind of weird."

Another time early in our affair, she said to me, "If you ever want that [meaning sex], I want you to know you can have it, but I also want you to know, I don't want it."

"Don't do me any favors," I said.

Looking back, I'd have to conclude that that was probably another regret. One of my favorite Kris Kristofferson songs is called "I'd Rather Be Sorry"*:

But I'd rather be sorry for something I've done
Than for something that I didn't do

Yeah, story of my life.

It got much weirder soon afterward when Rita also became involved with one of our male teachers. Terence, who was twenty-seven, married, and had a little baby girl. He was considered a wunder-kind in logic, and we both had him for the class Symbolic Logic I. Oh, and he was a sexual sadist heavily into bondage and discipline. Oh yeah,

---

* Written by Kris Kristofferson and Rita Coolidge

it got really weird, really fast, but it took me three years to finally get up the strength to leave.

By that point, I was no longer invited (nor permitted) to sleep with Rita, and I think the final blow fell when we were waiting in a vacant classroom for Terence to finish up a lecture he was giving in the classroom next door, and I was charged with "keeping Rita company" until they could leave together.

"This is so unfair to me," I said to her.

She shook her head slowly and said, "I know."

"Then let me go," I pleaded.

"I can't," she whispered softly.

And I knew that whatever else "obtained" (the common term for a conclusion in symbolic logic), she cared deeply for me and that it would be up to me to decide when to muster the courage to break away, to abandon something I would've given my soul to have to myself, but something that clearly was not meant to be. It was fascinating, stimulating, and, at times, I'd go so far as to say euphoric—yet flooded with anguish and heartache.

The night before my painful departure from Los Angeles, Rita came over to the little San Fernando Valley guesthouse I was sharing with my friend Barbara. We were watching television late into the night, avoiding a final farewell. An old movie was playing, and a commercial for some kind of crisis center came on. After it was over, Rita turned to me and said, "Did you get that number?"

"No," I replied. "I thought you got it."

Barbara, knowing full well the subtext, shook her head and observed, "You know, you really do deserve one another. You're both nuts."

I remember telling Rita, that fateful last evening, that I knew in a few short days I'd be walking down Fifth Avenue in Manhattan where, only a year earlier, I'd shopped at Tiffany's for a thin gold chain to give her as a Christmas present, and I said, "I'll be looking at all the faces I pass by and I know for certain that the only one I want to see will not be there, but still it's the only one I'll be looking for."

Before I ever met Rita, I attended classes at Pierce Junior College in the San Fernando Valley, hung out with friends, worked part-time at Sears in the catalog pick-up department, and drove back and forth across the country. I frequently qualified my life experiences as a prelude of sorts. I often thought to myself: *When my Real Life begins. . . .*

Well, I never thought that way after Rita. After that, there was no doubt in my mind—although it was agonizing, totally absorbing, occasionally exhilarating—life was now very, very real. Yes, I could write a whole separate memoir around it. In fact, I could write ten, but that journey, that long, painful, frustrating trip, whatever else it taught me, gave me an enormous amount of information about myself and the world I occupied. And also about how that world perceived me and how I perceived myself. It also taught me much about longing, loss, and unrequited love. That difficult journey was very different from the one that brought me back to Hydra and to Marianne.

So, I finally left Los Angeles and spent the winter living with my mother and sisters and working in the library in Kearny, New Jersey. Once I had enough money saved for several months abroad, I vowed to put miles and memories between the irresistible Rita and me. On the train traveling from Gatwick Airport to London some months later (before going to Greece), I wrote her this poem:

> We were never lovers
> Neither were we friends.
> Caught between the covers
> Of course, it had to end.
> You said you didn't want me

But you couldn't let me go.
Now you're still here to haunt me.
And you never let me know
If your life is full or hollow
If you've finally turned gay.
So, I take another swallow
And I dream my blues away

I left for Europe after three months of working. I traveled across the continent with a male cousin who was on his first journey overseas. When we arrived in Rome, he received a letter through American Express from his twin brother, who'd also attended college with us. This brother worked part-time at Sherman Oaks Hospital, which was quite famous for having the most advanced burn unit in the country. In the letter, he shared some very shocking news: My former old logic teacher and archrival for Rita's affection, Terence, had been in a very serious car accident on the Ventura Freeway. He was rear-ended by a delivery van, and his car's gas tank had burst into flames. He had to be pulled out through the windshield and was very badly burned. Initially, he was not expected to survive.

Instinctively, I knew how devastating that must've been for Rita. I had exactly enough money left to afford a one-way ticket from Rome back to Los Angeles, and my first impulse was to fly to her side to comfort her and be her support as I so often had been just months earlier. It was not an easy decision to make.

As we traversed Rome, stopping at all the famous sites, we approached the Trevi Fountain. There, I knew my decision had been made. I took off the ring I was wearing, the one she'd given me on my last birthday—two silver bands tied in the middle in a knot. (Yeah, I know—an interest in logic wasn't the only symbolic thing we shared.)

I turned my back on the historic fountain, and I threw the ring in over my shoulder just as I'd seen tourists do with the famous three coins.

I continued on my journey, feeling just a little bit "free at last."

We took the train down to Brindisi, on the heel of the boot of Italy, and crossed the Adriatic to the beautiful island of Corfu. And then on to Athens and, finally, after my cousin had flown back home, out to my new destiny: Hydra.

One day while sitting at Tasso's café on Hydra, with a friend, a tourist from one of the day boats asked if he could buy us two young girls a beer. Over conversation, it emerged that he was interested in finding out more about the island's ambiance.

"Isn't this the . . . 'Gay Island'?" he asked.

My friend laughed and answered, "No, that's Mykonos."

"What are the foreigners here then?" he inquired.

"Undecided," was her answer.

I remember nodding in agreement. "Undecided," I affirmed.

Back in the days of sex, drugs, and rock and roll, that was so true. With a few notable exceptions, no one's orientation was taken for granted on Hydra. One's past was never considered a confirmation of one's present or future attraction or behavior. There was a certain refreshing freedom in that attitude. One could judge each relationship not by a given person's sex, or age, or nationality but by the person: him or herself.

As disappointed as I was by what transpired (or didn't) between Marianne and me, I so enjoyed all the rest of the people and events on Hydra that it was sometimes difficult to remember that I was heartbroken. After all, as the saying goes, "tomorrow is another day."

So I passed the remainder of the summer. When I was finally, really, departing for home, I asked George, "What will I do when I have to return to a life which lacks ambiguity?"

"Don't worry," he said. "You won't."

The end of August arrived, and once again, I bought a ferry ticket. This time, my new friend Felicity left with me, and there was no fond farewell with Marianne at the dock, no profession of love or regret about what had failed to happen. Still, I was bereft to be leaving this place, the special atmosphere, and a bunch of incredible people whom I loved. When we boarded the ferry and walked to the rail to watch the island disappear, Felicity said to me, "I wish I could pick you up and throw you back, you look so sad to be going." She later mailed me a copy of a poem she'd written about leaving Hydra together that year. It's still one of my favorites.

Leaving with Judith

We jingle down Donkey Shit Lane,
Singing the songs of our friends.
Packs on our backs once again,
Early sun bright,
Been up all night,
Is it goodbye we can't comprehend?
Few people down at the port,
The corner café is deserted.
A picturesque summer resort
With just one to wave
Which helps us to save
Our feelings from being diverted.
We come here for our peace of mind
While Tasso says "It's all illusion."
More seekers are what we find,
And every life

Is edged with a knife,
And everyone leaves in confusion.
Such a beautiful day to depart,
Hot morning sun shining brightly.
The subtle town plays her part
To tempt our return,
(Will we never learn?)
As all of her houses smile whitely.

—Felicity Fanjoy, Hydra, August 1973

When we arrived in Athens that afternoon, we went, as always, to collect mail at the American Express, then went up to John Zervos' house to wait for our three a.m. charter flight which would take us to London. We'd caught the seven a.m. ferry to Piraeus after staying awake all night saying goodbye to everyone, and then, as luck would have it, we got no sleep at John's house because friends from across the street also came over to bid me farewell.

When we arrived at English customs, I was a total wreck and must've looked like just the kind of homeless, penniless hippie that England was doing everything to avoid allowing entry. I'd unwisely left my return ticket to the United States at my friend's house in Cambridge, so when we landed, the officials almost didn't let me through customs. Felicity and a guy we'd met on the plane came over to where I'd been told to wait and snuck some money into my hand. I was made to sit there until everyone else had cleared customs, and I kept wondering, *What are they going to do? Make me tread water in the English Channel?*

And then, in what must've been a bit of British irony, the officials stamped my passport with a one-year admittance visa—the longest I've ever been allowed on one trip. So off we went to attend the Cambridge Folk Festival.

I first met Brandy Ayre while he was living in a basement apartment off Sloan Square in London. I was given his contact info by a mutual friend, Charlie Gurd, who was from Montreal and had subleased Leonard's house there on Rue Saint-Dominique for a while. Charlie left Hydra some time before I did and had invited me to stay with him and his pal Brandy when I got to London.

Brandy was a poet and singer/songwriter, and he was also a friend of Leonard's from Montreal. He was tall, over six-foot-two, and very handsome with a sensitive face and an engaging personality. He was also a very gifted musician and a terrific singer. He'd been a part of the Montreal crowd on Hydra and had only left just before I arrived earlier that year. He was planning to spend a year living and working in London.

Anyway, I called the number Charlie had given me when I arrived in England, and Brandy told me Charlie was not there. He'd gone to a Buddhist monastery in Scotland to meditate. "Oh rats," I said, or something to that effect. When Brandy found out I'd come directly from Hydra, he kindly invited me to stay with him.

We hit it off immediately. We walked to a pub on the King's Road that evening, had a pint, and talked for hours about our lives, our loves, and, of course, about Leonard Cohen and Hydra. Brandy had hung out quite a bit with Leonard, and they often chatted about music and songwriters. Brandy told me Leonard claimed Jacques Brel was the best singer/songwriter in the world: "Ah Brandy," he'd said. "Brel? No one can touch him. He is just the best!"

I stayed with Brandy for several weeks and accompanied him to a number of clubs where he'd play and entertain. One in northern London was called The Round House. He also worked for a time as a session musician, and I got to go with him to the Apple Studio, which was still owned by the then-disbanded Beatles. Even though it had been three years since the Beatles' break-up, there was still a gaggle of young girls hanging out in the alley where the studio entrance was, hoping to catch sight of one of them or of anyone famous.

When we both returned home that year, me to New Jersey and Brandy to Montreal, we kept in touch, and I drove up with some friends to visit Brandy. He was living with his parents at the time in the town of Mount Royal, a Montreal suburb. His father was a doctor, and his mother kept a really lovely home. It was a large, white, stately-looking house, very neat and attractively furnished. Virtually every wall in the two-story place had artwork of all kinds hanging on it.

Years later, when I had my own house, I decorated it with as many different kinds of prints and posters and photos and even some original art (mostly from Hydra artists), and I told Brandy, when he came to visit, that his mother was the inspiration for my decorating choices. His mother was a rather formidable, Patrician-looking lady but was very kind-hearted if she liked you, and she took a real interest in me. It was a lovely visit, and I remained in touch with them for quite a while.

While I was staying with them that time, Brandy took me to a bar/café called Le Bistro where Leonard used to hang out. It was one of the few clubs where both French and English Canadians could be found together. The walls were covered with people's writings, poems, messages, notes, and observations. He showed me where Leonard had once written:

Oh Marita, please come and find me, I'm almost thirty.

Brandy and I could (and did) wax eloquent in endless discussions of Hydra and its personages. One night, out with a group of his friends, we started to apologize for going on and on about "our island," but they only urged us to continue. I guess our enthusiasm was contagious.

Brandy observed, "Hydra is like a drug; you become addicted to it."

Back in the United States late that summer, I stayed with my sister Cindy and my cousin Stephen who were renting a house at the Jersey shore. It was right on Barnegat Bay in the Silverton section of Toms River. I got a job waitressing at a place called The Top of the Mast in South Seaside Park and quickly resumed the mantle of a partying, working, drinking Jersey girl.

That fall, now settled back in New Jersey, I saw in the paper that Leonard Cohen was going to be performing at The Bottom Line in Manhattan. As it turned out, Rita was now living in Greenwich Village with a noted philosophy professor from USC named John Taurek. I was still trying to come to terms with our relationship but happy to see her.

Here's a journal entry from that time:

What Rita and John share in common, I have recently realized is an inclination towards fastidiousness. John already is, I think, fastidious beyond an acceptable degree. It goes further than the endless meticulously constructed inquiries into what makes the tea taste funny and applies, instead, finally, to basic important definitions, like "What is love?" I refuse to consider that it is only my resentment, which naturally accompanies the suspicion that Rita can relegate all her emotions for me into some lower designation like "special feelings," which causes my uncontrollable recoil from such an abstractly exacting regard for such questions. It seems to me to be an intellectual subterfuge, patently dishonest and designed to order reality in a way not yet manageable by even the best of us. In fact, it is fastidious to the point of being effete. Must love always be a consequence of good behavior? Is it always to be defined in terms of reward and punishment?

So with Rita in tow, I attended the show and, afterward, went backstage to the dressing room to say hello. I'd brought the photos I'd taken that summer, at his house and George's, of him and Axel and Marianne. There was one from her birthday that was particularly arresting.

Marianne stood with a red flower tucked into the front of her blouse, backlit against the setting sun, in a long black skirt and a white peasant blouse. Her features were almost in silhouette against the sunlight. She looked both mysterious and yet totally exposed. Leonard stared at that picture for several minutes before handing them all back to me. I tried to talk him into going out for a drink with us, my very attractive friend and me, but he pled exhaustion and turned us down.

I felt a little disappointed. We'd gotten on so well on Hydra, and it took me a long time before I realized that he was back in his "Montreal Life"; back with Suzanne and Adam, and Suzanne had just announced she was pregnant again. (I'm pretty sure she set out to get pregnant as soon as Leonard returned from staying with Marianne in Greece.) So he'd chosen which life he was going to stick to, or maybe fate had chosen it for him. And Hydra had to remain, for quite some time, just a chimera. A lovely memory.

Marianne confided that she'd gotten pregnant several times during her relationship with Leonard as there was no birth control available in Greece in those days, but each time, he would say, "It's not a good time, Marianne." Her pride left her only one choice. Ending the pregnancies was her only alternative. She confessed to me (and also mentioned in a book called *Love in the Second Act* by Alison Gold, a Jewish author from New York and a longtime Hydra habitué who owned a cottage in Kamini): "I couldn't give him Jewish babies . . . and Suzanne could."

(Although Suzanne claimed to be Catholic and was educated at Catholic schools in Florida, she was actually Jewish by birth, at least that's what Marianne told me.)

Marianne also told me another surprising thing about Suzanne's campaign to obliterate her from Leonard's life and completely usurp it. She said that Suzanne's birth name, the one she went by until she met Leonard, was Susan. She'd changed it to Suzanne so that everyone would think he wrote the song about her although he'd written it several years before he even met her about a completely different woman.

There is another lyric that I think evokes those choices:

She moved her body hard against a sharpened wooden spoon,
she stopped those endless journeys of going to the moon*

One time, Leonard spoke to me of his devotion to Roshi, his Zen master. When he mentioned to Roshi his feelings of displacement and torn loyalties, Roshi told him, "Just live your life, Leonard. Don't worry so much. Have children [although Roshi had none]. Just live! Everything else will be all right."

"Maybe you should do the same thing," Leonard told me.

"When you get back to Los Angeles, go see the Roshi." He sometimes called him The Roshi. "He will straighten it out for you."

So when I returned home to Los Angeles later that year, I tried to do just that. I called the Zen Centre on Vermont Avenue in downtown LA and asked to speak to The Roshi. The person who answered the phone took my number and said, "He will call you back."

And he did, the next day. The problem was—it was the wrong Roshi.

When I mentioned Leonard's name and said Leonard advised me to contact him, Roshi seemed puzzled. "I don't know this man," he said.

Now I was puzzled. "He didn't study with you on Mount Baldy?" I asked.

---

* from "Death of a Ladies' Man"

"Ah," he replied. "That is a different Roshi. He teaches at the Buddhist Monastery on Mount Baldy, and I teach here in Los Angeles. But come. Come down and visit. Maybe I can be of help to you."

Having nothing to lose, I made an appointment and, later that week, drove down to the Buddhist Centre. But I had some difficulty finding it and arrived about a half hour late. I knocked on the front door of the old Victorian-looking house, but there was no answer, so I walked around to the back. On the back porch, there were twenty pairs of shoes neatly lined up in two rows. The back door was open, so I slipped off my own shoes and stepped inside.

It was very quiet, and from one room, I could hear some chanting going on. I walked over to the door of the room, which was open a bit, and inside, I saw the owners of the shoes sitting cross-legged on the floor with their eyes shut.

Somehow, I knew this was not my scene, so I put my shoes back on and left.

I never returned to that house and made no other attempt to contact the "right" Roshi.

Letter to Marianne, dated Sepember 28, 1973, transcribed (see figs. 1a–1h)

30 Rutland Ave.
Kearny, NJ 07032
28 Sept. 1973

Dear Marianne,

Enough is enough! Greetings my friend, how are you? I've received reports from different sources which indicate you're not well. No one seemed to have any definitive information, however, so I'll have to continue under the assumption that it is nothing truly serious and that you are recovering quickly (I sure hope so, man!).

Felicity came down from Montreal last week and is now staying in New York City with Diane (who stayed on Hydra with Dimitri). I was up there on Monday and Tuesday, and we met Kim and Justine for dinner (at a Greek restaurant called "Idra"). They are doing well, and Kim (who is now called Bartholomew [dumb!]) mentioned that he had sent you a get well card and included my regards. Somehow I found that really depressing, you know?, you're receiving my regards from Kim, and I realized I'd be <u>more</u> than depressed if the games I occasionally indulge in (don't we all) to divert myself ultimately came between me and a relationship I truly value on a much higher level particularly since there are very few people who I come across in my life who I recognize to be outstandingly fine and worthwhile, and you are unquestionably one of them. So I can only hope as I write this that you are still aware of how much unqualified affection I feel toward you and that these feelings still possess the ability to have some effect on you.

You revisit me in so many strange ways, Marianne. Witness this; I received several communications from Felicity. And in one, she recounts a rather long and convoluted story involving a confrontation between her and the man who sub-leased your loft in N.Y.C. (this took place in Montreal) it seems he was carrying around and flaunting at his leisure a box of old photographs of you and Leonard and Axel, and during the course of one evening, gave one to Felicity. She, for reasons of her own (albeit very generous ones), felt I was more appropriately deserving of it and so sent it to me. I wonder if I can convey to you the sensations that I had while sitting here in Silverton, New Jersey, gazing at a ten year old photograph of you and Leonard, walking gleefully hand in hand through the port of Hydra, but it was absurdly tender and touching in any case. Felicity subsequently managed to obtain the entire box of photos from this man (who she describes as execrable) and has made some attempt to return them to Leonard. Speaking of Leonard, I have not seen him since my return, but did talk to him briefly on the phone several weeks ago—I'd seen advertisements for the opening of his play in N.Y. and wrote him that I intended to attend and inquired if it was possible to meet him at that time. He called and we agreed that an opening night was too hectic for any involved conversations, so I am supposed to let him know the next time I have time off and am going to the city. As it turned out the opening night performance was sold out, so I attended the night before (it was in previews) with Rita (which is another <u>long</u> story which I think I will spare you until I am reassured that you still have some interest in this correspondence) who is planning on spending the coming year in N.Y.C. I enjoyed the play very much and found some of it <u>very</u> surprising, as I think you will. It ends with an open letter to you from Leonard, and you know, it's funny, even though I read all (?) your mail, I found myself wanting to stand up and say "Shhh! That's somebody's mail, for Chrissakes!" I would love to see it again with you, but in any case, you <u>must</u> see it!

Leonard enquired by the way, when I spoke with him, whether or not I'd heard from you.

I receive mail from Jane and from George (since I'm paying her now for the sketch I bought) and am currently in the midst of preparations for my return to L.A. (are you still going to be there?).

Which will be by way of Montreal and Western Canada and shall commence within 2 or 3 weeks.

I will be in N.Y. again the beginning of next week and will attempt to reach L. again. If for any reason you want to get in touch

9-23-1973 first letter to Marianne after return from Hydra Fall 1973

I

30 Rutland Ave.
Kearny, N. J.
07032
28 Sept. 1973

Dear Marianne,

Enough is enough. Greetings
my friend, how are you? I've received reports from different
sources which indicate you are
not well. No one seemed to have
any definitive information, however,
so I'll have to continue under
the assumption that it is nothing
truely serious, and that you are
recovering quickly (I sure hope
so, man)

Felicity come down from Montreal,
last week and is now staying with (in New York City)
Diane (who stayed on Hydra with
Dimitri). I was up there on Monday
and Tuesday, and we met Kim and

Figure 1a.

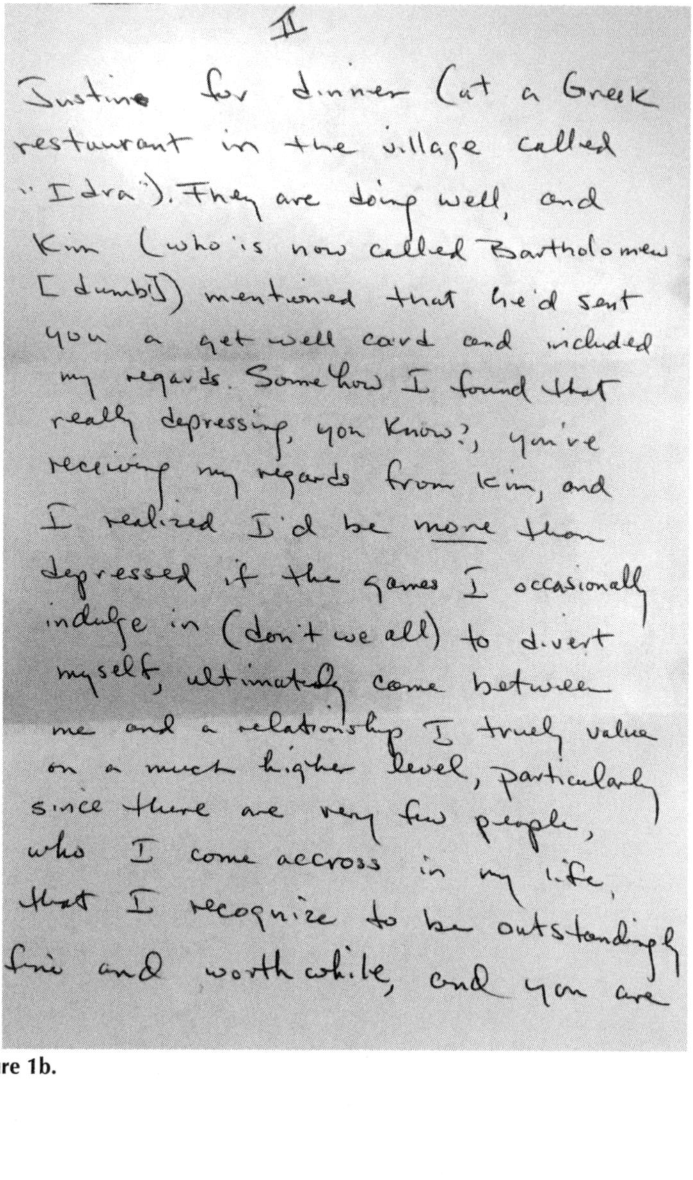

II

Justine for dinner (at a Greek restaurant in the village called "Idra"). They are doing well, and Kim (who is now called Bartholomew [dumb!]) mentioned that he'd sent you a get-well card and included my regards. Somehow I found that really depressing, you know?, you're receiving my regards from Kim, and I realized I'd be more than depressed if the games I occasionally indulge in (don't we all) to divert myself, ultimately come between me and a relationship I truely value on a much higher level, particularly since there are very few people, who I come accross in my life, that I recognize to be outstandingly fine and worthwhile, and you are

Figure 1b.

III

unquestionably one of them. And so
I can only hope as I write this,
that you are still aware of how
much unqualified affection I feel
toward you, and that these feelings
still possess the ability to have
some effect on you.

You revisit me in so many strange
ways, Marianne, witness this: I've
received several communications from
Felicity, and in one she recounts
a rather long and convoluted story,
involving a confrontation between her
and the man who sub-leased your
loft in N.Y.C. (this took place in
Montreal) it seems he was carrying
around and ~~flaunting~~ flaunting at his leisure
a box of old photographs of
you and Leonard and Hazel, and

Figure 1c.

IV

during the course of one evening,
gave one to Felicity. She for
reasons of her own (albeit, very
generous ones) felt I was more
appropriately deserving of it, and
so sent it to me. I wonder if
I can convey to you the sensations
I had while sitting here in Silverton
New Jersey, gazing at a ten year
old photograph of you and Leonard,
walking gleefully hand in hand through
the port in Hydra, but it was
absurdly tender and touching, in
any case. — Felicity subsequently managed
to obtain the entire box of photos
from this man (who she describes
as execrable) and has made some
attempt to return them to Leonard.

Figure 1d.

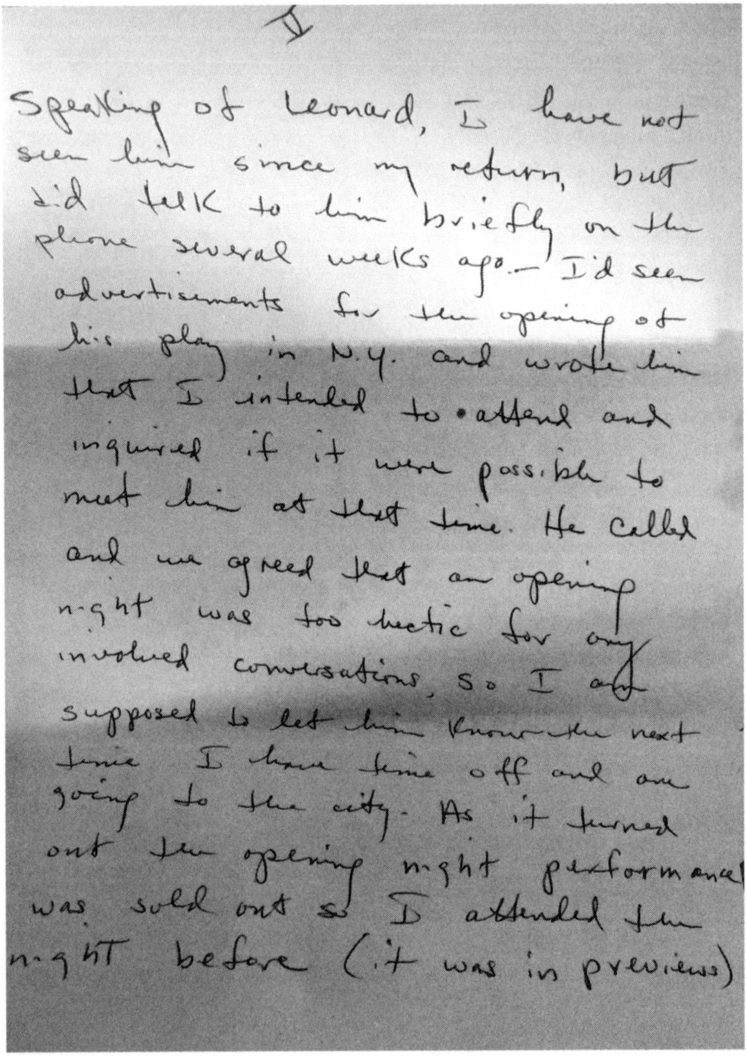

II

Speaking of Leonard, I have not seen him since my return, but did talk to him briefly on the phone several weeks ago. I'd seen advertisements for the opening of his play in N.Y. and wrote him that I intended to attend and inquired if it were possible to meet him at that time. He called and we agreed that an opening night was too hectic for any involved conversations, so I am supposed to let him know the next time I have time off and are going to the city. As it turned out the opening night performance was sold out so I attended the night before (it was in previews)

Figure 1e.

with Rita (which is another
<u>long</u> story which I think I
will spare you until I am reassured that you still have some
interest in this correspondence)

who is planning on spending the
coming year in N.Y.C. I enjoyed
the play very much and found
some of it <u>very</u> surprising, as
I think you will. It ends with
an open letter to you from Leonard,
and you know it's funny, even
though I read all (?) your mail,
I found myself wanting to stand
up and say "Shh! that's somebody's
mail for Chrissakes!" — I would

Figure 1f.

vii

love to see it again with you,
but in any case, you must see
it.

Leonard enquired by the way,
when I spoke to him, whether
or not I'd heard from you

I've received mail from Jane
and from George (since I'm paying
her now for the sketch I bought)
and am currently in the midst
of preparations for my return to
L.A. (are you still going to be there?)
which will be by way of Montreal
and western Canada; and should commence
within 2 or 3 weeks.

I will be in N.Y. again the beginning of next week and will
attempt to reach L. again. If

Figure 1g.

for any reason you want to get
in touch with me right away,
my home phone is: (201) 999-5310
and my address is on front.

If you are up to it (one way or
another) please write back soon,
as I will be on the road approx.
1 mo. after I leave, and please
take care of yourself baby —

love,
Judith

P.S. Please give all my
love to your incredible son Abel
PS: Don't show this letter to anyone!
(HA!)   over ⟶

Figure 1h.

with me right away, my home phone is: (201) 997-5310 and my address is on front.

If you are up to it (one way or another) please write back soon, as I will be on the road approx. 1 mo. after I leave, and please take care of yourself baby–

Love,
Judith

P.S. <u>Please</u> give all my love
To your incredible son Axel

P.S. jr. <u>Don't</u> show this letter to anyone!
(HA!)

Letter to Marianne, dated January 3, 1974, transcribed (see figs. 2a–2e)

Marianne,

Was relieved and gratified to receive your card. Actually it was mostly my fault about the letter, as I departed without leaving a forwarding address, and it will probably be there when someone goes to open the bungalow in the Spring then pirazi (is that even close to the Greek?).

1-4-74

Sorry I got interrupted by some company, and it is now tomorrow. I just talked to Ruth on the phone, and she said she is planning on writing you this weekend and would urge you to come to L.A. I understand the situation at this time presents a few more difficulties, with regard to employment and a place to stay etc., and so if I reiterate my offer of hospitality it is not just out of the selfish desire to see you again, but to alleviate any hesitation you might feel in arriving a stranger in strange place. Come and stay as long as you like. The house is relatively small but adequate. The job scene is not as bleak as you may imagine—one can always pick up something like a sales job at a department store until more suitable employment is procured. Whatever you do, get out of Oslo, it is disturbing to imagine you stuck in that morgue. California is sunny, warm, and easy on the soul.

Got a letter from George yesterday—I don't know how much to recount to you as I'm sure you must receive news from Hydra yourself and I don't want to be repetitious—but he says Christmas was nice—big party Xmas eve at Chinese Richard's house, and New Year's Eve party at Dimitri's. Layton stayed only one week and was George describes "as distant as ever." Leonard fine but doesn't see him too often as I guess you know Suzanne's sister is also staying there and to quote G. "Suzanne's sister does not look particularly interesting and I don't have with them the affinity I had with our darling mischievous Marianne" (mischievous? I don't know if I agree exactly the term, but I think I know what he means!).

Jane is back from the States and she is still planning on coming here but doesn't know when.

That's about all.

My life here is rather quiet—although of course I go out carousing with friends all the time—and they are only too happy to pay my way as my employment won't begin until February. But I think they are friends to me as Jane is a friend to you on Hydra—okay to be with when solitude becomes boring but not terribly stimulating, you know? In fact, I think as I write this that I am grateful for not having to recount to you my day to day activities, as I feel we are removed from the obligation of speaking about mundane things because we share no mutual reference on that level, and can for better or worse expose other parts of our experiences.

I still think often of this summer, and Hydra, particularly in contrast to the kinds of things I'm doing, and not doing lately. I'm so bored with people who demand and seem satisfied with nothing more from me than my presence and an occasional bright remark—there is nothing worse than performing for people who only appreciate the obvious. I have been thinking that the content of any experience is meaningless until you find the correct form, the proper interpretation (the one which reality requires) and conversely the form or interpretation of any experience is dependent on the quality of the content. In that respect I understood even when leaving Hydra the last time, why you were so angry with me when I departed, not because of anything I had done to anyone else but because of an intolerable lack of faith in myself, a momentary faltering in a situation that demanded resoluteness. If I had any complaint to harbor it was on another more ego-central level—on that one I had to face full responsibility. I wonder if ends cancel each other out? anyway, I'll find something interesting again pretty soon, I always do and write this only so you can commiserate with me—I'm sure you must find yourself often in similar circumstances.

Rita is somewhere in L.A., but as I told her <u>again</u> that I don't want to see her <u>again</u>. I don't know where—I sometimes wonder how much we are willing to inflict on one another (in general) in order to avoid being bored. (I wonder if Leonard ever asks himself that?)

Anyway, my can of Coors (beer) and I having completely exhausted all creative potential (possibly even all coherent potential)

1·3·74

Marianne,

Was relieved and gratified to receive your card. Actually it was mostly my fault about the letter, as I departed without leaving a forwarding address, and it will probably be there when someone goes to open the bungalow in the spring then peraci (is that even close to the Greek?)

1-4-74

Sorry I got interrupted by some company, and it is now tomorrow. I just talked to Ruth on the phone, and she said she planned on writing you this weekend, and would

Figure 2a.

I

1-3-74

urge you to come to L.A. I understand the situation
at this time presents a few more difficulties, with regard
to employment, and a place to stay etc., and so if I
reiterate my offer of hospitality it is not just out
of the selfish desire to see you again, but to alleviate
any hesitation you might feel in arriving a stranger in
a strange place; Come and stay as long as you like — the
house is relatively small but adequate. The job scene is
not as bleak as you may imagine — one can always pick
up something like a sales job in a dept. store, until
more suitable employment is procured. Whatever you
do, get out of Oslo, it is disturbing to imagine you
stuck in that morgue. California is sunny, warm
and easy on the soul.

Got a letter from George yesterday — I don't
know how much to recount to you as I'm sure you
must receive news from Hydra yourself and I don't
want to be repetitious — but he says Christmas was
nice ·big party xmas eve at Chinese Richard's house,
and New Years Eve party at Dimitri's. Layton stayed
only one week and was George describes; " as distant
as ever". Leonard fine, but doesn't see him too often,
as I guess you know Suzanne's sister is also staying
there and to quote G. "Suzanne's sister does not
look particularly interesting and I don't have with

Figure 2b.

them the affinity I had with our darling mischevious Marianne" (mischivous? I don't know. if I agree exactly with the term - but I think I know what he means! Jane is back from the states and he is still planning on coming here but doesn't know when. that's about all —

My life here is rather quiet - although of course I go out carousing with friends all the time - and they are only to happy to pay my way as my employment won't begin until Feb. But I think they are friends to me as Jane is a friend to you on Hydra — okay to be with when solitude becomes boring but not terribly stimulating, you know? In fact I think as I write this that I am grateful in not having to recount to you my day to day activities, as I feel we are removed from the obligation of speaking about mundane things because we share no mutual references on that level, and can for better or worse expose other parts of our experiences.

I still think often of this summer, and Hydra, particularly in contrast to the kinds of things I am doing, and not doing lately. I am so bored with people who demand and seemed satisfied

Figure 2c.

with nothing more from me than my presence
and an occasional bright remark — there is
nothing worse than performing for people who only
appreciate the obvious. I have been thinking that
the content of any experience is meaningless until you
find the correct form, the proper interpretation
(the one which reality requires) and conversely the
form or interpretation of any experience is dependant
on the quality of the content. In that respect
I understood even when leaving Hydra the last time,
why you were so angry with me when I departed, not
because of anything I had done to anyone else, but
because of an intolerable lack of faith in myself,
a momentary faltering in a situation that demanded
resoluteness — If I had any complaint to harbor
it was on another more ego-centred level — on that
one I had to face full responsibility. I wonder if levels
cancel each other out? Anyway, I'll find something
interesting again pretty soon, I always do — and write
this only so you can commiserate with me as I'm
sure you must find yourself often in similar circumstances.

Rita is somewhere in L.A. But as I told her again

Figure 2d.

that I don't want to see her again - I don't know where. - I sometimes wonder how much we are willing to inflict on one another (in general) in order to avoid being bored. (I wonder if Leonard ever asks himself that?)

Anyway my can of Coors (beer) and I having completely exhausted all creative potential (possibly even all coherent potential) are signing off now - I'm going to see a skin flick (porno movie) tonight and some friends who you would like - but not love -

Love,

Judith

P.S. Got a letter from Axel - short and sweet but was good to hear from him . hope Xmas was good for you - take care baby -

P.S. again - saw your friend David Blue's name in the paper - guess he's still playing around town.

Figure 2e.

are signing off now—I'm going to see a skin flick (porno movie) tonight with some friends who you would like but not love.

Love,
Judith

P.S. Got a letter from Axel—
Short and sweet but was good
to hear from him, hope Xmas was
Good for you—take care baby—

P.S. again saw your friend David Blue's
name in the paper—guess he's still playing around town.

Another letter to Marianne, transcribed (see fig. 3)

Los Angeles
21 Feb, 1974

Dear Marianne,

Sitting here in the California sun listening to David Whiffen, wondering where in the world you are, and how you are, if everything is okay. I could be completely wrong, but I get the feeling if all was well, you would have written back by now. I don't know how much consolation one person can be to another, across ten thousand miles and after several months, only know I have the inclination to try. (Survival of the fittest?) Be well,

Love,
Judith

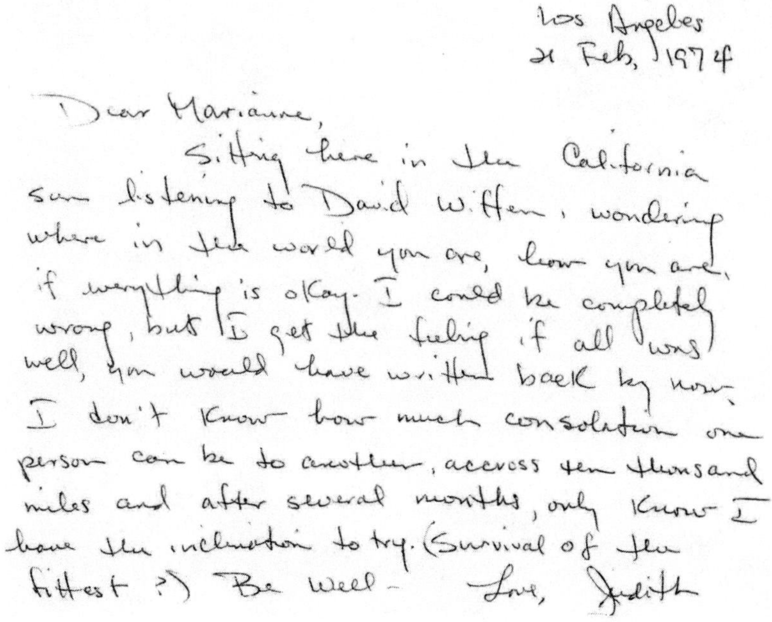

Los Angeles
21 Feb, 1974

Dear Marianne,

Sitting here in the California sun listening to David Witten, wondering where in the world you are, how you are, if everything is okay. I could be completely wrong, but I get the feeling if all was well, you would have written back by now. I don't know how much consolation one person can be to another, across ten thousand miles and after several months, only know I have the inclination to try. (Survival of the fittest?) Be well — Love, Judith

Figure 3.

2

1975

All through 1974, after quitting college again and working in New Jersey at a clinical lab, I longed to return to Hydra. I'd heard that Marianne was there (although she'd had an illness and returned for a time to Norway to get an operation). I couldn't wait to see her. The falling out after I left in 1973 was still a fresh wound. I did something that, in retrospect, I probably shouldn't have.

I was into writing poetry back in those days, and I wrote a poem in late 1973 about Marianne and my time on Hydra with her and Leonard. Having seen Leonard in New York in the fall of 1973, when he performed at the Bottom Line, and spoken to him several times on the phone after he returned to Montreal, I sent it to him. Here it is:

For Marianne

I am feeling strong and proud today,
Because I haven't written to you.
I've put my shared compassion for anguish,
Apprehension and wrinkles
Into a box marked "Hydra,"
And have taken to staring blankly
Out at the bay.
(Also, I still drink.)

All power struggles between individuals
Derive from the desire to obtain
Commitment without reciprocation
That you got easily with one brief movement:
"You don't have to sleep so far away"
And one short phrase:
"I can't while he is in the house"
And so propelled me into
A strange fraternity
(Too late to make any impression)
It is not just our love they crave,
But also our hate;
Not feeding on emotion, but on energy.
This is not my style, I know.
These are not my words,
But that's okay, I told you
I wasn't very original.
I am feeling strong and brave today.
And I did not write this poem
Out of love or even resentment,
But from a long-standing affair
With justice.
It's silly. . . . There is no way to end it.

—Judy Scott, Toms River, NJ, 1973

I never heard back from Leonard about it, but sometime later, I was intrigued and delighted to hear a fragment of that poem in one of Leonard's songs. More on that later.

At last, I could resist the lure of Hydra no more.

In the early summer of 1975, Brandy Ayre took the bus down to New Jersey where I'd purchased two charter tickets for Belgium, and off we headed, once again, to Greece. We shared a hotel room in Brussels. Then he took a train directly to Athens while I flew to London to visit with my good British friends back in Cambridge.

I still loved Cambridge; it's my favorite English city. I'd been punting on the Cam and was a frequent patron at the Fort Saint George pub, which sat right on the banks of the river. In front of the "George" was a large village green, which connected to the main street in town. In the middle of the green was a lovely, old-fashioned, wrought-iron street lamp with beautiful glass bulbs pointing in all four directions. Around that time, someone had scribbled "Reality Checkpoint" on the bottom of the post where it connected to its support.

(When I returned to Cambridge after my six months on Hydra that year, I asked my friends if the message was still there, and they told me the town had paid to have the base of the lamppost painted with those words in different colors, and "Reality Checkpoint" was now official— now, that's my kind of town.)

After attending the Cambridge Folk Festival with my Brit friends, where I so enjoyed the performances of John Prine, Steve Goodman, and Stéphane Grapelli, from Cambridge, I bought yet another student charter, and two weeks later, I was back on the island. I knew Brandy had intended to rent a house as soon as he got there, so I walked through the port looking for someone who might tell me where he was.

At Tasso's, I saw Chuck Hulse and Gordon Merrick, a famous gay author (the couple was part of the Hydra elite crowd) sitting with, of all people, Richard Branson of Virgin Records. They told me that Brandy had rented the house where George and I had taken the acid trip, and Branson said, "Give Brandy my best; I'm going to make him a star one of these days." Brandy was signed for a while by Virgin Records and was going to record an album for them, but for one reason or another, nothing ever came of it.

I somehow managed to find his house way up high near the "new" cathedral and was happy to discover Brandy at home. I dumped my stuff there and went off to see if George was at home as well. This time I'd remembered to tell George I was coming but didn't send him a specific date, so when I got to his place and an unfamiliar young American girl answered the door, I was a little dismayed to find out that George was traveling on Mykonos with his new German girlfriend, Angelika.

The woman at the door was named Marilyn. She was from Seattle and had been staying with George for almost a year. She described herself as his housekeeper. Also, there was Skip Milson, an American man who was an old friend of George's and had lived in Kamini for a while some years before. Skip taught at the Boston Museum of Fine Arts, in their Art School, and was an inspired artist himself.

They knew nothing of my arrival, so I went back and stayed with Brandy until George returned a week later. Then I moved my stuff over to George's once again, and the four of us (Angelika had had to return to her shop in Germany) made a pleasant little household. We all loved Hydra, and we all loved to cook and were pretty good at it, so we'd take turns shopping and preparing dinner every fourth night. We each made very different types of food, so it was an arrangement we all enjoyed.

Being a night owl, one thing that is hardest for me to remember when it was my turn to shop was, back in those days on Hydra, the island, like most other locations in Greece, completely shut down during the afternoons. All the shops, the grocery stores, butcher shops, outdoor fish market, even the tourist shops (if there were no tour boats in the port), closed from one p.m. until five p.m. And all the inhabitants, Greek and foreigners alike, took a "siesta." You dare not phone anyone or try to stop by during the "quiet hours." It was mainly due to the fact that Greece came very late to modern air-conditioning, and it was ungodly hot during the summer afternoons. One of my housemates would always have to remind me, "Judy, you'd better get down to the port before the shops close or you'll have to take all of us out to dinner!"

Before he left for India with George that summer, Skip gave me a charcoal drawing he'd done of the port of Hydra at three a.m. He told me, "Nobody deserves this more than you Judy, because nobody has spent more time in the port at three a.m.!" (I was pretty sure Skip had developed a little crush on me.) That framed sketch still hangs in my upstairs hallway.

While staying with Brandy for ten days until George returned, I slept in a small bedroom just off the kitchen in the house he'd rented. It shared a wall with the big new cathedral (well, actually just a large church), and my bed was right up against that wall.

I was not particularly religious or a spiritual seeker (twelve years of Catholic schooling and four years studying philosophy tends to have that effect). My closest friends on Hydra—George, Leonard, and Marianne—were far more interested and involved in spiritual and/or mystical teachings than I was. However, I did have two spooky, quasi-spiritual experiences while there.

One night, I returned about three a.m. after a typically bibulous evening and, as I was dozing off, heard a rhythmic chanting coming from the church right behind my head. Having sung in a choir as a student, I was very familiar with Gregorian chants, and that's what it sounded like. But the thing is, I could also "see" the monks doing the chanting. There were about twenty of them, all attired in the dark brown vestments that monks like Friar Tuck commonly wore, with cowls pulled up over their heads. Somehow, this vision did not shock or frighten me, and I drifted off to sleep, feeling strangely comforted by the sonorous choruses coming from next door.

I recounted this episode years later while dining with the Brownings, more Hydra habitués. Robert Browning (yes, a descendant of the poet), a retired British foreign-service officer, and his wife, Audrey, were very involved in all kinds of mystical speculations and even hosted seminars on such things. They were fascinated when I told them about the chanting monks. They assured me that what I'd had was a vision, a magical peek into a fifteenth-century ritual, as no such ceremonies or group of monks had ever existed on modern-day Hydra.

Another time, in late Fall 1975, late at night, when I was returning home from a small dinner party in the Neogi house a little further up the mountain from mine, I approached a sharp right turn in the path. On one side was the main east-west upper-transverse road; on the other, a steep drop-off into a ravine. The wind was howling that night, and the electricity was out on the island (a fairly common occurrence, especially when a strong wind was blowing). I was alone in the dark, and I got a very strong intuition that heavenly creatures (not entirely friendly ones) were about to make an appearance. It was such a powerful impression that I addressed the darkness out loud.

"Listen," I said, speaking into the chasm. "Whatever it is you want to impart or confirm, this is really not a good time for it!"

The sensation gradually dissipated. With only the light from my torch (i.e., flashlight—an essential item when traveling at night on Hydra), I got back to my rented house and into my bed as fast as I could. I could feel my heart pounding as I hid under the covers. Although, as usual, I had imbibed a fair amount of wine, I remember that strange perception vividly, even to this day. It wasn't just the wine.

Oh—and I almost forgot: George's house was said to have two resident ghosts: a young peasant girl and a very disapproving Greek priest. Some things are just taken for granted on Hydra. Although I never really saw them, I often had the feeling that I'd just missed catching sight of them a couple of times.

Once again, my anticipated reunion with Marianne was not to be. Jesus—this carrying-a-torch thing was getting to be ridiculous! Marianne had left the island two weeks earlier, leaving fifteen-year-old Axel behind at the house—which was now occupied by Suzanne. Suzanne was there with Leonard's four-year-old son, Adam, and eleven-month-old daughter, Lorca. There was also a crazy Algerian nanny and her four-year-old son.

I don't remember my first meeting with Suzanne; I guess it was probably through Axel. He'd been relocated from his longtime bedroom (now Adam's room) to the downstairs studio—which was much larger but felt like an unfinished basement. Anyway, I spent a fair amount of time with Suzanne, and though I tried to like her, I found her to be a very cold and vain person. At one point, she said to me, regarding the children, "I'm really not that into being a mother. Leonard is far more interested in the children than I am."

I remembered from that first summer in 1973 Leonard saying of her: "I don't think she knows how to be a mother." At the time, there was only Adam, who was then two, and Marianne had answered, "Send him to me then. I'll take care of him."

Suzanne was attractive, I guess, though not my type. She was small-statured and slender, but she was the most voracious eater I'd ever met. She positively inhaled food! In fact, it seemed to me that every time I joined her in the port, she was consuming something.

Not long after I arrived, the young, gay clothing designer Richard Tam (who was from a wealthy Chinese family in San Francisco) and his beautiful blonde boyfriend (I think his name was Gary) decided to host a costume party. It was the height of the summer, and everybody who was anybody in the ex-pat community was invited.

The theme was One Thousand and One Arabian Nights, so everyone had to come in an appropriate costume. George had a big trunk in his library, and from its interior, he extracted costumes for all four of us. He provided me with a dazzling pair of multicolored silk trousers and a beaded vest; for Marilyn, a belly dancer's skirt and top; for Skip, a turban and long-flowing caftan; and for himself, the outfit of a pasha.

Richard's house was just to the right of Madame Pauori's, high on the hill to the left of the port, with a lovely arched veranda in front and a swimming pool in front of that. All the rooms were beautifully decorated, and the bedrooms had fluffy white clouds painted on the ceilings. The party was going to be the event of the season. I was so glad to have been included.

As we all walked there through the port (George's house was to the right side, on the opposite hill), we encountered Helen Marden and Suzanne. Their costumes were something I will never forget: Helen had on beautiful, brown, chiffon pajamas and no top—just an open jacket and balloon pants, and she had oiled her breasts with a deep metallic-copper glaze.

Wow. (And I must admit they were spectacular breasts.)

Suzanne had on . . . well, I don't remember what kind of clothing she wore because that was pretty much obliterated by the giant aluminum-foil penis she'd constructed to wear around her waist as a cincture. Double wow! I can't remember if there was a best-dressed contest that night, but I'm sure if there was, they would have won.

For some reason, Suzanne decided during this visit to change Adam's name. She told everyone she knew to call him Noah from then on. What I really got a kick out of was—no one would! We all kept calling him Adam, until finally she gave up.

But there were two related incidents that kind of set my opinion of her in stone (and not in a good way).

About a month after I was back on Hydra, she decided to go to France to search for a house to rent for the winter. She was leaving the children with the au pair, who by now seemed to everyone to be less than equal to the task. I saw Suzanne in the port just before she left, and she told me, "In case there is an emergency, I've given the key to the phone [an old rotary-dial black one] to Deidre, because I don't trust [what's her name, the au pair] with it, so she can only take incoming calls."

I thought to myself, *How incredibly odd—she can't trust her with the phone, but she'll trust her with her two young children!* But there was worse to come.

About two weeks after Suzanne left, Axel, with whom I'd been spending pretty much every day, came to me and said, "I got some mescaline. I want you to take it with me."

"Oh Axel, do you think that's such a good idea?"

"I've got some, and I'm going to take it," he answered, "whether you take it with me or not. But I'd like you to."

I knew that Axel had had hashish before but nothing stronger, and I wanted to make sure he'd be okay, so I reluctantly agreed. Truth be told, I had a fondness for occasional psychedelics myself, so I said, "Okay, but we're just going to stay in the house, not go anywhere else, deal?"

"Deal," he agreed.

That night, I arrived at the house after the kids had been put to bed, probably about nine. The au pair, as per usual, was down at the port drinking. We took the drug, made some tea, and sat down to talk. We were sitting on the cot in Leonard's studio, the one made famous on the back cover of *Songs from a Room*. I don't remember everything we talked about, but I do remember speaking of the influence and effect that Leonard had had on both of us—me, mostly from a distance, and Axel very up-close. I remember Axel saying, "He's almost like a ghost. He's always somewhere in the background."

"I know, Axel," I answered. "Others know the song, but we [pointing to the open window], we know the wire."

Around midnight, the au pair returned, quite drunk, with two chubby French men from one of the yachts in the harbor.

"There!" she exclaimed. "There is the desk. I told you this is the room of Leonard Cohen."

She reached for the album, which was standing in the corner of the room with a stack of records. "See!" she said. "Here is the picture of this room, and that—that is Marianne's son!" She pointed at Axel. "Say hello to them, Axel!"

We pretty much stared in horror, and Axel remained silent. Both men looked uncomfortable, and I thought they needed a reason to escape. One of them asked if there was anything to drink in the house. As the answer was no, they beat a quick retreat.

The au pair sat in a chair and addressed Axel again. She had a very low, gravelly voice, almost like a snarl. She was not in a good mood.

"So when is she coming back, do you know? Has she told anyone? The money she left is all gone. I can't buy food for the children! She has not called, not even once! They won't give me any more credit at Four Corners. I had to ask the Greek maid to loan me some money. I'm getting out of here as soon as she gets back. They don't treat you good here! And you, Axel, why are you still staying here? She doesn't want you here! And he"—pointing toward Leonard's desk—"he doesn't want you anymore either. He has his own son now. He doesn't need you. He doesn't love you anymore! Who stays in your bedroom now, eh? It's not your room anymore!"

I could feel Axel's muscles tense in his arm where it touched mine.

"No response, Axel," I whispered. "No response."

She continued her rant, "They use you, then they throw you away! Just like me! What do you have to say to that?"

Axel tensed again; I could see the muscles in his jaw set tight. We both just stared at her, saying nothing. Finally, she waved us away, "Ah, you're useless. I'm going to bed." And she left us, sitting there, quite stunned.

Finally, after a short time, I said, "For this, he cannot be forgiven."

Axel replied, "Do you mean that?"

"Yes, I do."

"I won't let you forget you said that," he told me.

I felt pretty traumatized myself and assured him, "I won't forget Axel. I won't forget."

And I vividly remember even to this day that awful night which might have been the beginning of Axel's long retreat from the world.

Shortly after this horrible evening, Axel came to me and said, "I'm in trouble."

"Okay," I said. "Tell me the problem, and we'll take care of it."

"I lost my return ticket, the one Marianne left for me. I want to go back home now, but I can't find it."

"Okay, don't worry," I said. "If we can't find it, I'll go with you to Athens and get another one." And though we looked everywhere for it, in the end, we took the boat into Athens, and I bought Axel another student charter ticket to Oslo for $75.00, and a few days after that, he was gone.

Suzanne still hadn't returned, and things looked like they were coming to a head at the house with the children. One night not long after Axel's departure, Skip and I went down to the port around midnight and went out to the disco, Cavos. The au pair was there and was once again quite drunk. We stayed very late, until almost six a.m., and when we left, she followed.

"Come down to the café," we invited her, "and let's get some coffee."

We guided her down the banister-less stone steps, a fairly precipitous climb even when sober, and walked back toward the part of the harbor where all the shops and cafés were located. At some point, she left our side and went toward a large monument located near the wide pathway. "Wait for me," she said and disappeared from view behind the statue. She had on a long cotton skirt and sleeveless blouse, and it was obvious she was intent on peeing. Then a few seconds later, she called out, "Go! Go on, don't wait for me now!" and we kind of knew that she had peed on herself.

We went to the nearest open café, Antonio's, and sat looking at one another. "We have to do something," I said finally. "This can't go on any longer. She'll never be in any shape to take care of that baby when she wakes up or of Adam either—and God only knows when Suzanne will return."

"Yes," Skip said. "We need to talk to George, and he needs to try and contact Leonard."

So back up the hill we went to the house, and later that morning, after a brief rest, we sat down to talk to George. He just shook his head when we told him what had happened and readily agreed that Leonard needed to be informed about the mess at his house and what was going on with his children. Leonard was, at that time, staying once again at Roshi's monastery on Mount Baldy just outside Los Angeles.

George pointed to me and said, "You can make the call. You know Los Angeles. Find out how to contact the Roshi and talk to whoever you can at the monastery."

I agreed, and we calculated that we'd need to wait until seven p.m. Athens time, which would be nine a.m. in Los Angeles. Later that afternoon, Skip went down again to the port to buy groceries for dinner. When he returned, he had some surprising news: Suzanne had gotten off the afternoon boat. She was back!

So Leonard was not contacted after all.

As one might guess, Hydra itself is a character in this story: a living, breathing entity. Therefore, I must say a few words about the flora and the fauna of the island.

Summer is naturally the most popular season on Hydra, but my personal favorite times are late spring and early autumn. In spring, the hills are alive, not with the sound of music, but with something even better—wildflowers. The winter rains always result in blankets and blankets of gorgeous wildflowers. Even the air smells sweeter, more alive, and all creatures, great and small, are energized. For a brief time, before the oppressive heat of summer, everyone walks around smiling, even the habitually grumpy ones.

I guess every kind of paradise has something like a serpent, though, and so does Hydra, two of them in fact: giant centipedes and tarantulas. The hill where my rented cottage sat and where George's house was also located was known for being an ideal environment for tarantulas.

Even back at the beginning when I first stayed at George's, I knew those buggers were around (and I'm very fearful of spiders). When the wine in George's two large barrels got below the level of the spigots, he and Skip called me and handed me a brick.

"Here," they'd say, "we will tip the barrels forward and you climb behind and stick this brick under the back of the bottom barrel."

Oh, how I didn't want any part of that! But how could I possibly refuse? I was staying in this gorgeous house for free and had very little in the way of chores. Also, being the smallest, this task was definitely destined to be my contribution to the household. I took the brick, climbed quickly over the supporting frame, gave the okay, and slid the brick under the wine cask as quickly as I could—with my eyes closed.

The next day at lunch, Skip mentioned casually, "I saw two tarantulas sitting on top of the wine barrels yesterday. I managed to kill both of them."

That was my first near miss.

Then there were the giant centipedes. They, too, were indigenous and fairly common on Hydra. And I'm talking really giant ones that were like eight to ten inches long.

Once, in 1973, when I was having dinner at Douskos with George and Leonard, I heard a strange noise, kind of a soft squeaking, like someone opening a rusty hinge or lifting a metal chain.

"What is that?" I asked.

George pointed to the ground. There, maybe ten inches from my bare, sandaled feet, was a creature I'd never seen before. It was a light pinkish-beige, about seven or eight inches long with a carapace so hard that it squeaked when it moved. Ignoring my leg, thank goodness, it moved past me and proceeded to climb the tree in the middle of the taverna.

I resisted the urge to scream.

George told me centipedes were a common pest, quite poisonous but not at all aggressive. "Just ignore them," George said, "and they won't bother you."

I spent the rest of the meal with my legs crossed on the chair and, from then on, always checked the area before sitting outside anywhere.

Marianne told me that, once, she got up in the middle of the night to get a drink of water and there was a giant centipede on her kitchen wall. Their shell is so hard, you can't really damage them by simply whacking them with a broom. It was just her and Axel at home, so (and I can hardly believe this) she took two water glasses that just fit over the front and back end of the centipede and drove them onto the wall and twisted them until the creature tore apart into two pieces. Those

Norwegians are a tough breed. I told her if it'd been me, I'd have just given it the keys to the house and left.

Gwen, the American who took care of the Kellogg house (a lovely old Greek house up Kalo Pigati owned by a divorced in-law of the Kellogg Corn Flakes fortune, Eva Kellogg) and let us stay there (the following year, in the fall of 1976), showed me a large scar she had on her arm: two parallel dotted lines running down the outside of her forearm. It seems that a centipede fell out of the reed-covered ceiling just over her bed while she was sleeping. It landed on her, and startled awake, she tried to brush it off. That's when I found out these buggers have stingers in each of their one-hundred feet. It gave her a good sting, and her arm blew up to three times its normal size. She ran a high fever and had to travel into Athens for treatment. Of course, she did kill that beast.

The other insects that caused much annoyance, but were not at all dangerous, were the cicadas. They seemed to be in every tree during the summer, and they made a terrible racket. Because it's so hot during the day, people usually take a siesta from around three until just past six p.m., and that is when the cicadas seemed to be at their noisiest. Although I understand they are related, their sound was nothing like a cricket's. As many people know, it's a high-pitched buzzing, incessant and very irritating. But, like the braying of the donkeys and the crowing of the roosters, it was something one simply got accustomed to on our little island paradise.

Hydra is also known as the "island of cats" and, although there are stray cats on most islands, they really populated Hydra because there were no cars or buses to run them over. The Greeks on Hydra tolerate the cats because they keep vermin from coming off all the yachts and ferries and delivery boats to infest the port. Also, they eat fish guts that the fishermen remove after their daily catch and discard on the harbor stones. Lastly, the cats, especially when young and cute, attract tourists to the various tavernas and restaurants.

Almost all of the foreigners had at least one pet cat and, usually, because there was no vet to spay or neuter the animals, they ended up with quite a few. Once, when I was visiting Christina Kingsmill (after she and Anthony had split up), one of her cats, just a year old, was discovered to be pregnant and about to give birth. Something quite remarkable took place.

Christina had prepared a bed in a cardboard box behind an upholstered chair in the corner of her kitchen, and the cat was lying in it, wailing like a baby. It was clear the poor creature had no idea what was about to happen to her. The cat's own mother, who also lived there, jumped on the chair, lowered herself behind it, and helped to birth the kittens. She also helped to clean them and bit through the umbilical cords. Hydra's cats had to be very resourceful, and this was a good example.

Almost every time I visited or lived on Hydra, I adopted or at least fostered a cat. The first one I became attached to was a kitten of George's cat, Boubulina. She was born while I lived with him in 1973, and I nicknamed her Flash Gordon because she'd fly into the living room and dash from sofa to sofa to counter to floor in a flash. When I returned in 1975, she was still there, but everyone warned me that she was no longer very friendly and would snarl and scratch if you tried to pet her. Well, not me. She remembered me and would sleep in my lap and purr like crazy when I stroked her. I was pretty sure Flash (or Flazz, as they called her in Greek) had just been pissed off that I'd left her and was very happy that I'd returned.

When I moved into the little house I rented from Lindsey, we ended up with three young cats. Tennis Shoes was named after a misunderstanding during a conversation with Mette Jakobssen (more on her later), where I was referencing the kitten in my arms and she was referring to a pair of lost tennis shoes. So, that became his name. Then, there was Sophie, a very young tabby with the softest fur and loveliest green eyes. And finally, there was Zara, whom Mette adopted and who drove me nuts because you couldn't get her to stop kneading your shirt when she jumped in your lap.

Lastly, there were the ubiquitous donkeys and mules. They were the true workhorses on the island because anything and everything taken up the hillsides to the many houses toward the top had to go on their backs.

Everything, from groceries to refrigerators, was hauled up by donkey labor.

The donkeymen took very good care of their animals while they were able to work, but one time, I heard about a small donkey who became too old to haul anything large or heavy, so the owner just stopped feeding it. This angered me. He wouldn't even waste a bullet to put it down. Oh, those Albanian Greeks can be a fierce and often unfeeling race.

Fortunately, the donkey managed, after several days of starvation, to get out of its enclosure and onto a pathway. But it was so weak it couldn't even make it to a patch of grass. A foreigner who lived on the island found it lying in the middle of the path and managed to rescue it. It carried his groceries for him and survived several more years.

There were the seven cats I was mandated to feed at the Kellogg house, but I never got really close to any of them. They stayed outside all of the time and hid under the house in the evenings. None of them had been given a name. They were as close to feral as Hydra cats could get, but they sure came running whenever I returned from the market with fish for them.

We always fed the cats congregating around the corner from Brian and Valerie's "up" house (the one we always rented), and on one trip, we adopted a cute little tabby kitten with a black slash under his nose. We named him Mustaki (Greek for "mustache"), and when we left after two months, we gave $75.00 to Anne Rivers—an eccentric writer from Texas who had lived on Hydra forever and who eked out a living taking care of foreigner's houses—to feed Mustaki over the winter, and she did.

When I returned to Hydra in 1975, besides being so happy to be remembered by Alexis, I was equally delighted to become reacquainted with and closer friends with Anthony Kingsmill, who was in his tenth year of living on Hydra.

Anthony welcomed me like a long-lost friend. "I can't wait to hear you sing 'Danny Boy' again," he told me. And sing it I did, but luckily for me, who would have felt pretty foolish belting out the Irish ballad in the middle of the port in the middle of the day, Anthony mainly requested it toward the end of our evening of eating and drinking together. I was genuinely worried, though, that it all might come to a calamitous end when I witnessed firsthand, one evening in the summer of 1975, what Anthony was capable of if he didn't like you.

I was sitting at a café in the port with Anthony when the newlywed husband of another Hydra habitué, a rich, very preppy-looking blonde-haired, blue-eyed fella from Back Bay Boston, sat down and joined us. I'd gone with him and his new wife to a small uninhabited island off the coast for an afternoon of swimming and picnicking just the day before. I guess the preppy fella thought that allowed him to join us, uninvited.

It didn't sit so well with Anthony. He asked the fella a few questions about his history and current employment, then started to excoriate him unmercifully.

"You think you're so special, with your navy-blue blazer and your penny loafers and your rich, superior airs!" Anthony virtually spat at him. "You don't have an honest bone in your body! You're nothing but a phony! You don't belong here, and you never will!"

On and on he went. I could see the guy's face become flushed and red. He looked at me in stunned and voiceless entreaty. I felt like I was taking my life into my hands, but I had to put a stop to this. I put my hand on Anthony's arm and said softly, "That's enough, Anthony. Stop it now."

I was seriously worried Anthony would turn his bile on me, but I couldn't let it go on any further.

"Oh, but darling," said Anthony, "he is quite a pompous ass!"

"That's enough, Anthony."

To my utter astonishment and relief, Anthony did stop. He turned away from leaning forward and glaring at the guy and muttered something under his breath. He didn't apologize or anything, just lit another cigarette, poured himself more wine, and sat back in his chair. His unfortunate victim used that pause to nod a quick goodbye to me and escape. I heard he and his wife divorced only three years later, and needless to say, he never returned to Hydra.

I'd brought a small amount of drugs with me from London. Some mescaline and hash, I think, and when Suzanne heard about it, she started hounding me to sell her some. After several entreaties, I finally broke down and said, "Okay, just give me what I paid for them and you can have the whole lot."

Many years later, I heard via the Hydra grapevine that when Suzanne returned to the island another time, she told everyone I was a drug dealer.

They got a big kick out of that.

I didn't.

Later that summer, Suzanne developed a passionate crush on a young French artist, Jean Noel, who was staying with friends in Kamini.

Unfortunately for her, he was gay. I remember how adamant she was about bedding him. She seemed quite sure that if he ever really experienced sex with a passionate, sultry woman, he would change his mind about being gay.

September 18, 1975

Yesterday, Suzanne rang up to ask if she could borrow the tape recorder. She wants to tape some music to take with her to the South of France. I brought it to her house, and she fixed us lunch. It's funny, every time I am with her, she is eating something. She eats very quickly and with strong concentration. She seems voracious to me. She told me she no longer wants to live in France but will spend one month there as she has already paid the rent up front. It is a six-bedroom villa with a swimming pool.

She asked me, "How could I have rejected Leonard for a young, gay French boy I no longer even like?" She continued, "I asked Leonard on the phone if he could forgive me, and he said, 'I don't know, I've made so many sacrifices on your behalf.'" I think that she is completely crazy, but maybe it is only that she is incapable of love (desire, yes, but not truly love). Each time I see her, we chat quite pleasantly and appear to get on well, but a voice in the back of my mind keeps saying, "Why, Leonard, why?" and I hear him respond, "Why should you care, Judy?" And I know it is an equally good question.

It struck me then, as I recalled what Leonard had said about sleeping with Marianne ("Sex with Marianne was always excruciating, but I desired her very much") that perhaps Suzanne—so visceral, so very sensual—was a much more compatible partner for him on a certain essential, physical level.

Right after I returned to Hydra in 1975, I spotted Alexis Bolens in the port having a beer.

"Hello," I greeted him tentatively. "I don't suppose you remember me."

"Oh, I remember you," he replied. "You're Black Bart's girl!"

We laughed.

On yet another occasion, while sitting in the port together, apropos of nothing, Alexis looked at me and said, "So, you had a little fling with Marianne."

I was a bit taken aback. "Why do you think that?"

"Has no one told you the Hydra motto?" he asked.

"No, what's the Hydra motto?"

He chuckled and said, "It goes like this: If you want to do anything on Hydra and get away with it, don't do it for more than an hour."

I had to laugh and concede, "Well, I loved Marianne very much, but I never slept with her."

"Really?" he asked. "Everyone thought you were sleeping together."

"Well, that time, everyone was wrong," I responded.

Alexis thought about this for a second, then observed, "More's the pity."

I nodded and ruefully concurred, "Yeah, more's the pity."

The longer I spent there, the more I realized that motto was very true. Without television or movies or much English-language radio (except for an Armed Forces station out of Hellenikon Air Base and BBC Worldwide News), gossip was the chief entertainment on the island—that and watching silly tourists. No matter how private one tried to remain, on Hydra, one's life was pretty much an open book.

Later that summer, Alexis and I were walking back to the port from the disco Cavos around three a.m. When we got to Kalo Pigati, where Alexis lived, he turned and asked me, "Would you like to join me tonight?"

Of course, I knew what he was suggesting. Colby was in Athens on business, and Alexis was not known for being the faithful husband.

"Pas ce soir."

He took it well.

"Quel dommage."

Bill Cunliffe was yet another very well-known Hydra ex-pat. He owned Bill's Bar, made famous in a song by Leonard, "The Night Comes On." Some of the lyrics concerned the group of us who hung out there:

I'll go down to Bill's Bar, . . . and I'll see if my friends are still there
And here's to the few who forgive what you do and the fewer who don't
even care

(Flash-forward to 1988 when the BBC did a special piece on Leonard returning to his house on Hydra. It is widely available on You-Tube. When Leonard first gets off the hydrofoil, he's greeted by two gentlemen, Bill and Alexis. He looks surprised to see Alexis there: "I didn't expect to see you here," he says. Then the three old friends walk through the port, and the camera crew follows Leonard up to his house.)

And so many of us did just as Leonard wrote in that song—we checked in at Bill's at least once a day. It was the place that all foreign residents went to for an early drink, to socialize, catch up on gossip, and make plans for the day and evening. Bill's Bar first opened that year, 1975, during my second stay on Hydra. Originally, it replaced a laundry that was just up the road from the port and was visible from it, where the Amalour Bar is now. Later, it moved into a space a little further up a side road in an old, abandoned sponge-processing plant. Bill was British, about my age, and married to a lovely Greek lady named Lena when he first opened the bar. (Bill was actually able to get a business license to open the bar because Lena was Greek and the license was issued in her name as business licenses issued to foreigners were very difficult to obtain on Hydra—the Greeks were not fond of competition.) They had two daughters, Kathy and Caroline. Bill lived for many years on Hydra, both before, during, and after his marriage. Inevitably, when he was broke and ill from way too much drinking, he would be forced to close the bar and return to England. A liver transplant lay in his future—but unfortunately, the transplant only prolonged the alcoholism that eventually took his life. I was present for many memorable occurrences at Bill's. One involved the gifted artist Dimitri Gassoumis.

That year, Dimitri was still living with his Australian girlfriend Deidre, whom I'd met my first time on the island, but like many of the regulars, Dimitri was having an affair. This was with another Aussie girl named Vickie.

One day, I happened into Bill's for a drink around eleven a.m. (the usual time) and found it filled with friends, Dimitri and Vickie among them. Everyone knew he was fooling around with Vickie—everyone except Deidre, that is. Bill's was not very big. It had a U-shaped bar behind which was the bathroom. We all watched (well, noticed) as Dimitri and Vickie discreetly slipped into the bathroom together. They'd been gone quite a while when, lo and behold, Deidre came in and asked the assembled, "Has anyone seen Dimitri?" We all looked surreptitiously at the door to the bathroom before we collectively shook our heads.

"No," we said, kind of sheepishly. "No, we haven't."

Oh God, I thought, *please, please don't let that door open now.* I'm pretty sure—no, I'm positive—that that was the collective prayer of everyone in there at that moment. If Dimitri came out, Deidre would know we'd all known where he was (and with whom). In fact, I think it was our collective angst-filled energy that kept the bathroom door closed.

After a few seconds, Deidre looked around and then commented, "He was supposed to meet me at Katsikas"—the grocery store—"but I can't seem to find him. If you see him, can you tell him I went home?"

"Yes!" we all eagerly responded. "We certainly will."

I've had some experience with group-think or group feelings (kind of like the mob-mentality syndrome) but never had I quite felt the unspoken group panic as when Deidre walked in and the sudden rush of relief we all felt when she walked out again. The scene that surely would have followed Dmitri's and Vickie's rank emergence from the bathroom would indubitably have destroyed a lot more than just the peaceful atmosphere.

After the summer crowds had departed, the rest of us settled in for the fall and winter. George had closed up his house and left for India with Skip Milson, and I'd rented a little house of my own nearby. I was privileged to be the only female invited to join Alexis, Anthony Kingsmill, Jean Marc, Dimitri, and Pandias Skaramanga, a wealthy Greek with a big house on the island who had been president of the Bank of Greece, at their weekly poker games.

During that winter, Alexis told me much about his former life. He had an incredible life story. Here's what I know:

He had been a mercenary fighting against the Mau Mau Uprising in Rhodesia and, afterward, had managed a coffee plantation in South Africa. He said that he once went two years without seeing another white person. Despite being political opposites, we developed a strange rapport. There are some people you encounter in life, I think, with whom you would never have imagined becoming friends, but some-how, something ephemeral, something almost spiritual, draws you to them.

Another person of note with whom I became friends (and still am) is George Dillon Slater. When I first met him in 1973, he was captaining a big yacht owned by a very wealthy man named Throckmorton who had a house on Hydra. Slater had a girlfriend living with him, a lovely lady named Diana.

George was tall and lanky with a chinstrap salt-and-pepper beard and mustache. He had a sun-weathered complexion and piercing blue eyes . . . well, really *one* piercing blue eye and a matching glass eye-ball due to an unfortunate incident—a bar fight in an Oakland dive, where he was hit across the face with a cue stick, and his left eye was completely destroyed. But that was in his younger days, though he still exhibited signs of a terrible temper when provoked. He was quite hand-some and had an engaging personality and a wicked sense of humor. He also was a bit of a Lothario and had had many lovers, among them Paloma Picasso and Nancy Farnsworth's daughter, Phyllis Major, a model who eventually married Jackson Browne.* He also had a short-lived but very passionate affair with Marianne during one of her many temporary pauses with Leonard. "We were going to run away to India," George told me. "I was staying with her at the house, and I thought everything was all set, then one day just before we were set to leave, she got word that Leonard was coming, and I was tossed out on my rear." He told me about this many years later. He didn't seem to have minded

---

* Sadly, Phyllis committed suicide when their young son was four, after suffering from depres-sion for most of her adult life. Browne channeled his loss and depression over her death into the production of his fourth album, *The Pretender*. Over the years, Phyllis wound up being the subject of at least three songs written by Jackson: "Ready or Not," "Sleep's Dark and Silent Gate," and "In the Shape of a Heart."

all that much; there were many fish in the sea back then, and George was an excellent fisherman.

I saw George and Diana pretty frequently during that period in 1975 and enjoyed their company. He made the very best curry I ever tasted and was also a very fine poet. I loved both his cooking and poetry.

Sometime during the fall of 1975, Slater and another rather infamous person, Sinclair Beiles (pronounced *Bay-liss*)—a South African madman who was William Burroughs' editor on *Naked Lunch* (and lived for a while in Burroughs' compound in Morocco)—gave a poetry reading at one of the local hotels—the Miranda, I think. Anyway, I went to it along with all the other ex-pats, and both poets were terrific, but what I remember most vividly is when Slater was reading his work. Beiles quietly got behind the chair George was sitting on and started doing somersaults. George looked genuinely puzzled when everyone laughed in what I'm sure he thought was a rather inappropriate response to his poem.

Another funny thing happened to George around that time. He kept going to the Hydra post office every day to check for his mail, as we all did. For weeks there was nothing for him in the "S" slot at Poste Restante. After a while, he noticed that another slot was getting quite full. "Whose mail is that?" he asked the girl. She produced the stack for him to look at and, sure enough, filed under "E" was a pile of letters addressed to George Dillon Slater, Esquire!

I didn't know Sinclair Beiles very well, but he was, of course, also a friend of Leonard's. He was a thin, short-statured man who came from a wealthy South African family, and I'd heard all kinds of gossip about him. He'd been institutionalized several times for depression. An eccentric such as Sinclair fit right in on Hydra in those days and probably still would today.

He and Slater published a book of poems together entitled *A Cathedral of Angels/LunaPark*, and I was very fortunate to receive a copy from Anthony, who had two. But Beiles and his lady friend didn't stay long on Hydra that time, just a couple of days.

At Thanksgiving of that year, Dimitri gave a big dinner party for all those of the foreign community. Dimitri had gone into Athens and brought back two large, dressed turkeys. I attended with George and his nephew, Constantine Zinnis. Constantine, who was George's older sister's son, visited George frequently while I was there. He was just about my age and was tall, thin, and avuncular-looking with big black spectacles. I loved to tease him because he took most things so very literally.

"Constantine," I would ask, "what does '*then exero*' mean?"

"I don't know," he'd reply.

"Oh, I thought you spoke Greek fluently!" I'd pretend to protest.

"No, no, Judy, it means 'I don't know.'"

Another time:

"Constantine, what does '*ti pota*' mean?"

"Nothing."

"Oh come on, Constantine, it must mean something," I'd insist.

"No, no, Judy, it means 'nothing.'"

Of course, I was already quite aware of what both phrases meant, but he was such fun to tease. Anyway, during that dinner, Slater got up and stood in front of the big buffet table in Dimitri's high-ceilinged studio and did one of the most extraordinary things I've ever witnessed:

He ate a wine glass.

The entire thing.

You could hear the crunching of glass as he chewed up the pieces and swallowed them.

George and Constantine were aghast. They said, "Judy, he's your friend, make him stop!" But he didn't stop, not until the entire goblet—stem and all—was gone.

When Slater and his present wife, Alice, visited with us years later, I asked him, "How did you do that? Was it some kind of group hypnosis?"

George just chuckled.

Alice demanded, "How did you do that?!"

"Just a little party trick I learned."

Apparently.

A very significant thing happened to me that year on Hydra—I got pregnant. It had all actually started back in 1973 when I met yet another friend of George's, Nisette Brennan. She was a young artist, a sculptor, living in Athens. Her father was in the diplomatic service—the Chargè D'Affaires at the American Consulate in Thessalonica—so Nisette had lived in Greece for quite a while and spoke very passable Greek. She used to stay at George's house from time to time, and when I went into the city, I would often go and visit her very quaint and funky studio and small apartment in the Anofiotika section of Athens just above the Plaka behind the Acropolis. When I returned in 1975, we resumed our friendship, and once I'd rented my own little place on Hydra, she'd stay with me there, and I would stay with her when I needed to be in Athens. On one occasion, Nisette's brother and two of his friends were visiting from Georgetown University in Washington, DC. We all went out together for dinner and Greek music, and I became friendly with her brother's college roommate, James. I invited all three of the boys to come and visit me on Hydra, but James was the only one who took me up on that offer. He stayed with me for about a month, and during that time, we became lovers, and I became pregnant. When he left to visit Israel and Egypt, he told me he'd be back in a month or so, and he did return, but I'm sure he was not expecting the news (at that point, only an increasing suspicion) that I gave him. There was no doctor or clinic on the island in those days, so after about a week, we decided to go into Athens to confirm what I was pretty sure was the case. That was an adventure.

I'd gotten the name and number of a maternity hospital and doctor who practiced there from mutual friends who assured me they'd do a pregnancy test for me. I called the number as soon as we arrived, and the doctor told me to come by the next morning.

So, early the next day, off I went by taxi while James waited in Syntagma Square. The hospital (Mitera Klinica—Mothers' Clinic) was bustling with people, some carrying flowers and fruits and some leaving with little bundles of joy. But there was no reception desk or admissions office. So, I wandered around the hallways, peeking in doors and asking in Greek if anyone spoke English.

Finally, at the Finance Office, a young woman came out to help me. I told her what I needed, and she brought me to the lab on the second floor. Fortunately, the tech in the lab also spoke English, but unfortunately, she informed me I couldn't have a test done without a doctor's prescription slip. I told her I was under the impression from friends that the test could be done as long as I had the money to pay for it. She just kept shaking her head.

"It's impossible," she kept insisting.

Feeling defeated, I mentioned that I'd spoken with Kyrie Kyriaki the night before, and he was the one who'd told me to come in the morning. Voila! Everything suddenly changed. "Kyrie?! Mister Kyriaki?!"—turns out he was not a doctor—"He is the head of the lab! Why didn't you say that from the beginning?" Right away, she gave me a cup to pee in and pointed me to the toilet.

Mission accomplished, she took the sample and said, "Call back here after three this afternoon, and I will have the results." Then she gave me a slip and took me to the cashier's office. I think it cost five bucks. I hopped in another cab (they were dirt cheap in those days) and met up again with James, and we sat at a café in front of the old American Express building at the bottom of Syntagma Square, waiting. I probably should've anticipated the results I was going to get because, for once, I didn't feel like drinking beer.

At the appointed time, I crossed the street to the public phone booth and made the call.

"Your test," the same girl said, "is positive!"

No doubt James was just as staggered as I was. He'd waited for the news but was on his way to the train station to leave Greece for Italy.

"Write and let me know what you decide to do," he said. Then he hoisted his backpack, and off he went. I caught the afternoon boat back to Hydra.

At one point that summer and fall, the little house I was renting got very crowded. Lindsey Callicoatt, the owner of the house (an amazing man—more on him later), had returned and asked if he could stay in the storeroom opposite the bathroom where there were both a cot and a small dresser. James and his friend Guy were there, too, as well as Philip, a friend of Marilyn's from Australia, who arrived for the summer and transmogrified into a very, very gay fellow.

Then, as summer drew to an end, within a week, I went from having a house full of roommates to being alone (though, perhaps with my secret pregnancy, one could say, not quite alone).

The off-season was definitely setting in. All the summer people and tourists were pretty much gone. Even the tour boats didn't show up nearly as often. The permanent foreign residents and those, like me, who planned to spend the winter there became much closer and spent more time together. I started having dinner regularly with Dimitri and his daughters, Athena (sixteen) and Cassandra (fourteen). Larry Hulse often joined us. He was the younger brother of Chuck Hulse, who lived with Gordon Merrick, the gay American novelist well known for writing *The Lord Won't Mind*, one of the first contemporary explicit books about a romantic homosexual relationship. Along with Leonard Cohen and Brice Marden (a world-renowned artist), Chuck and Gordon were members of the ex-pat elite. But they had decamped to Sri Lanka for the winter, so Larry was alone in their big house with its indoor pool.

October 12, 1975

The atmosphere right now in the house is peaceful and friendly as we are all locked in our private kingdoms of useful activity, but the underlying vibes when we emerge are wearing on everyone's nerves. The emotions are too various and too intense and bounce off each other like we were stanchions in a pinball machine, exhausting us and making us long for sleep or drink or, finally, the holocaust of confrontation. All are good people, but the house is too small for six seekers at a time. Three, I think, would be the ideal number.

October 13, 1975

Everyone in the house is working. Lindsey and Guy and James are filling the newly made flower box with dirt so grapevines can be planted. Philip is doing the dishes (his mannerisms more feminine day by day—he was nothing like this when he first arrived, an ex-boyfriend of George's American housekeeper, Marilyn). It is a curious but common Hydra phenomenon. Another ex-pat, a sweet guy named Kim Clark, went from being a shy singer/songwriter to hanging out with all the gay boys and changing his stage name to Bartholomew Neddings. Mette cannot stand to be around Philip now.

She made a very nice Norwegian breakfast today, which she insisted I get up and share even though she knows I never eat in the morning. The problem there surges and recedes. I make love with James in a disinterested and haphazard fashion across the room from her little bed, separated only by a stone partition (yet he tells me if the situation in the house were different, he'd remain here longer with just me), while I long for her body with a desire and intensity which shocks and confounds me. I have no idea where it will all end and this indecision will contribute enough energy to propel the scene toward some resolution.

James has a similar attraction to Lindsey (as did Brandy in the past) with the same fatal hesitation: "I wouldn't mind if you slept with him," I said. "No, I didn't think you would," he replied, "but I just don't know." Because it is more aesthetically pleasing for him to imagine two women together, the difficulties lie on another level. I can see that if part of what I enjoy is the violation of a taboo, so Lindsey must be even more attractive to him as it is even more forbidden. I do not envy anyone else their problems but wonder why this island elicits them in so straightforward and unavoidable a fashion.

November 1975

I wondered what in God's name I expected to find down at the port. Probably no one there on a Monday night, but I went anyway and had a good time after all. I found Dimitri, Anthony, Christina, Cassandra, Athena, Emily, Christo, and Philemon all in Graphos, and we stayed there, moving later to Brantley's, until two-thirty in the morning. Dimitri showed Anthony how to play a simple little gambling game while Athena and I served as referees. Each had to guess how many coins the other

Judy Scott, taken by Leonard Cohen on his terrace, Hydra, 1973.

Judy at Three Brothers Taverna on Donkey Shit Lane, Hydra, 1982.

Judy on the boat to Hydra, 1973.

George Lialios in his garden, Hydra, 1973.

Loading luggage on donkeys. Photo courtesy of Charlotte Gusay.

Judy's friend Susan Watts on Donkey Shit Lane, Hydra, 1982.

Axel Jensen and Felicity Fanjoy, Hydra, 1973.

Greek thousand-drachma note.

Photo of Judy taken by Leonard on his terrace, Hydra, 1973.

Judy lighting Marianne's birthday cake, Lialios living room, Hydra, 1973.

Leonard and Axel goofing off in the Cohen kitchen, Hydra, 1973.

Leonard Cohen and his cat, Edward.

Leonard Cohen relaxing on his terrace, 1973.

Leonard Cohen sunbathing on his terrace, 1973.

Jean Marc Appert, Hydra port, 1975.

Adam Cohen and Suzanne Elrod, Hydra port, 1975.

Steps to the swimming rocks, Hydra.

Hydra swimming rocks, "Montreal Beach."

Rita V. Lewis, Los Angeles, 1971.

Judy, Terrence, and Rita, Los Angeles, 1971.

Marianne on her birthday, May 18, 1973.

Brandy Ayre, Hydra, August, 1975.

Judy and her kitten, Flash, on the Lialios terrace, Hydra, 1973.

Lindsey Callicoatt in his courtyard, Hydra, 1974. Photo courtesy of Lindsey Callicoatt.

Alexis Bolens and his wife, Colby, Hydra port, 1975.

Alexis Bolens, Hydra port, 1975.

Lunchtime in the port, 1974. L-R: Mikalis Maniatis (Greek actor), Cassandra Gassoumis, Suzanne Elrod, Richard Tam (designer), Dimitri Gassoumis, Ed Tuttle, Deidre Dowman, Valerie Lloyd Sidaway, Christian (friend of Ed Tuttle), George Chakiris (actor), Gary Craig (boyfriend of Richard Tam). Photo courtesy of Valerie Lloyd Sidaway.

Dimitri Gasoumis and Deidre Dowman, Hydra, 1975.

George Slater giving a piggy back to Marianne, Hydra, 1967. Photo credit George Dillon Slater.

Helen Marden and Leonard Cohen en route to George Slater's wedding, Hydra, 1976. Photo credit George Dillon Slater.

Judy Scott and James Torrenzano on the Callicoatt terrace, Hydra, 1975.

Athena Gassoumis, unknown friend, Dimitri Gassoumis, Axel Jensen, Hydra, 1975. Photo Courtesy of Valerie Lloyd Sidaway.

Athena Gassoumis, Hydra, 1975.

Mette Jacokssen on the Callicoatt terrace, Hydra, 1975.

Athena Gassoumis, Hydra port, 1975.

Mette Jacobssen on "our terrace," Hydra, 1975.

Jeff Brown and Marsha Picaud, Hydra port, November, 1975.

Marianne and Axel, Oslo, 1976.

Axel Jensen in his apartment, Oslo, 1976.

Marianne in her apartment, Oslo, January, 1976.

Judy at Marianne's apartment in Oslo, January, 1976.

Judy and Torie on the Kellogg Terrace, Hydra, 1976.

Judy and Torie, Los Angeles, 1980.

Angelika and George Lialios,
Hydra, 1982.

Anthony Kingsmill and Torie Scott,
Hydra, 1982.

Charlie Gurd, Hydra, 1982.

Jean Marc Appert and Anthony Kingsmill, Hydra, 1987.

Anthony Kingsmill, Jill Appert, and Torie
Scott, Hydra, 1987.

Valerie and Brian
Sidaway, Sherri
Jacobssen, Hydra, 1990.

Judy and Monika, Hydra, 1990.

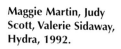

Maggie Martin, Judy Scott, Valerie Sidaway, Hydra, 1992.

Lindsey Callicoatt, Hydra Port, 2006.

Alex Carswell and Harold Ramis,
Montreal Beach, Hydra, July, 1973.

Lindsey Callicoatt, Anne Ramis,
Meri Lobel, and Harold Ramis (in
background), Hydra, 1973. Photo
courtesy of Lindsey Callicoatt.

Lindsey Callicoatt on his terrace,
Hydra, 1976. Photo courtesy of
Lindsey Callicoatt.

Lindsey and Judy at the Marden
House, Hydra, 2008.

Judy and Marianne, Melina
Mercouri Gallery, Hydra, 2011.

Judy, Marianne, Brian and Valerie Sidaway, and Jan Stang, Hydra, 2011.

Signed title page of Leonard Cohen's *Book of Longing*.

LEONARD COHEN

to Judy
with love
leonard

Book of Longing

Los Angeles December 2009

Judy and Marianne on her birthday, Lialios terrace, Hydra, 1973.

Marianne's birthday bouquet, Hydra, 1973.

pulled from his pocket up to a maximum of three. It was truly delightful to watch these two talented artists playing and guessing over and over like a couple of kids.

Athena and I had a pleasant conversation. We reflected on the summer people and what a bunch of phonies most of them were. I told her about a book I had found long ago in a Sausalito bookstore, a small book of poetry and photos published locally that I had never been able to find again and was so sorry I hadn't purchased at the time. It had such a striking title: *I AM A LOVER AND HAVE NOT FOUND MY THING TO LOVE* (which is a quotation from Sherwood Anderson, but he was not the author of this booklet). Athena really liked the title. We also talked about being a believer and what faith can mean. And she told me she had received a letter from Marianne. Altogether, a nice serendipitous evening.

I returned to my little home to find the three cats I had temporarily adopted, Tennis Shoes, Sophie, and Zara, arranged in an attractive bundle on the chair right in front of the heater. It had started to pour rain again, and I hated to think what their lives would be like when I left in three weeks.

I sat down to write and then got to musing. I used to think that loneliness and solitude were interchangeable concepts; then I learned how to feel lonely in a crowd, and now the other side of the coin presents itself. I am in love with solitude!

The rain started again today. I stayed in the house all day, and Cassandra, Dimitri's younger daughter, who is fourteen, came by and stayed for about an hour. We had a cup of tea. She is so very different from Athena I cannot believe they are sisters. It is rather difficult for her here. There are very few children on this island, and she will always risk comparison with her older, more outgoing, much more beautiful sister.

November 1975

The rain finally stopped after three days of downpour that saw another familiar face depart. Jean Marc finally left after all the delays and postponements. It was just the day before a gorgeous Thanksgiving at Dimitri's: turkey, stuffing, mashed potatoes, cranberry sauce, creamed onions, the works! Who says you can't eat well on the Greek Islands?! Everybody in attendance looked lovely. There were twenty-one of us, including Dimitri, his daughters Athena and Cassandra, Brian and Valerie, Deidre, Michael, his au pair Janet, Chuck and Gordon, Larry, Alexis and Colby [Kobi], George Slater and Diana, Jim and Leslie, Vivi and Vibe, Jeff, and me. Some of them I knew well, and some I didn't know at all.

The next day, Brian, Valerie, and Deidre left for Singapore and then on to Australia. Brian and Valerie are returning home after ten years abroad. Who knows when we'll meet again? And then yesterday, my "family" Vivi, Vibe, and Jeff left together to hitchhike to Copenhagen where I'll join them in three weeks.

Last night I shared a dinner of leftovers with Dimitri and his daughters. After the meal, I finally had a talk with Dimitri which felt pretty comfortable. He is such a hard man to get to know. And later, sitting around their kitchen table with Athena and Cassandra, laughing about silly things, made me feel really homesick for my kitchen and my own sisters. It made me wonder if that will ever happen again with them.

And another journal entry a few days later:

Today has been such a sweet day. Irresistible. One filled with solitary, simple housework pleasures from the first moment when I sat on the upstairs terrace of my little house, drinking my morning coffee, examining and enjoying once more the beautiful panorama of this island: the houses, the incredible blue of the Aegean Sea with the Peloponnese peninsula in the background.

Everything was made more poignant by the realization that my time here, the number of clear blue mornings on this terrace, is drawing short. I've only got a few more weeks of this bliss.

After my coffee and contemplation, I got to work clearing the mess accumulated over the previous five days of carelessness. I threw the bowlful of onionskins (from the creamed onions I'd cooked and contributed to the Thanksgiving feast) out the window into the compost heap. I threw the cooking water reeking of onion over the wall as well because the sink drain is broken and ends up delivering water into the bedroom of my closest neighbor, so now everything must go out the window and into the heap. I fetched fresh water from the bathroom shower, the only room connected to a hot water tank, and put two pots on to boil. I scrubbed the plastic wash basin inside and out, organized dirty dishes, silverware, etc., and began to clean them. It's ridiculous to be so pleased with myself for finally getting around to such a basic everyday job. But the warm, soapy water felt good, and the sun was streaming into my window over the sink, filtered by the green leaves of the apricot tree which overlooks the downstairs garden patio. I scrubbed the two-burner petro-gas stove, the refrigerator, and the table. It is a beautiful kitchen table, solid oak with round turned legs, which could easily seat six. I spend a lot of time here. I found a clean, white, but rather old and tattered table cloth, then arranged the salt and pepper, orange earthenware saucer which serves as an ashtray (though I myself don't smoke, never did), and the unfired-pottery sugar bowl in the middle of the table. I put David Whiffen then Simon and Garfunkel and Melanie on the little on-its-last-legs record player and sang along in sheer contentment. In the bathroom sink, I soaked four pairs of underwear and one pair of navy-blue socks.

Finally, ready to eat at last, I stuffed a tomato with tuna salad and fried up an omelet with vegetables and lots of good melted Greek cheese. I carefully set the table with one white plate, a knife, a fork, and a glass of tomato juice and began rereading Lawrence Durrell's Balthazar *while I ate, but I couldn't stop humming an old Vandekamp pork-and-beans jingle: "Simple pleasures are the best!" I didn't even pause to consider the incongruity, but I did pause to notice the sunset which comes early these days, around five o'clock, out of my kitchen window. Everything was delicious, and I remembered to boil another pot of water for the dishes while I ate. Finished and feeling almost too content, I gave the remaining fish from the fridge to the cats and put some water on to boil for coffee in my beautiful one-cup, blue-enamel Greek coffee pot with a long handle and built-in spout. I made dark, rich Nescafé and drank it with condensed milk and sugar followed by a sweet and juicy tangerine. One candle burned in the four-pronged holder suspended over the table, and a muted electric light with a dried-flower-covered basket as a lampshade lit my reading material. Dishes done, I made out tomorrow's grocery list. Then I couldn't decide whether or not to go down to the port for another cup of coffee and maybe a cognac, but it was still early, only nine p.m.*

If life had only days like this to offer, I'd be stir-crazy in a week. But if it didn't have one every once in a while, I'd be done before I started.

There's no mention of my pregnancy in these journal entries, though it was definitely on my mind. It was not really something I wanted to work through in a journal. Maybe I felt the journal was my last refuge, the place to forever preserve my happy Hydra memories before the responsibilities of adulthood permanently asserted themselves.

In any case, I hadn't decided yet what I was going to do about the situation.

December 1, 1975

This may just be the first day of my life I did not speak to or see another human being. What's most surprising is the curious equanimity of my mind. I feel my inner-self motionless, aside from the absurd pleasure I derive each time I regard my clean, orderly kitchen!

    My project for today was a big pot of fresh vegetable soup which sits invitingly on my stove. Bay leaves, garlic, a few drops of olive oil, George's homemade curry powder. It smells and tastes delicious! Living here is living so close to the skin—chopping vegetables while listening to the sound of my own voice singing old songs like Eydie Gormè's "How Did He Look" and her husband Steve Lawrence's equally lovely "The Ballad of the Sad Young Men." I'm ridiculously content. I started reading One Hundred Years of Solitude *by Gabriel García Márquez. This seems like a particularly appropriate time for this book.*

    The Norwegian twins Kari and Mari left today. I forgot they were going until it was too late to go down to the port to say goodbye.

The "elephant in the room" makes an appearance here:

December 9, 1975

Some sun again today, the rain seemed to go on forever. Yesterday I saw something outstanding! A beautiful rainbow, the biggest and best I've ever witnessed, started in the port and went all the way up to the monastery on the top of the mountain behind the town.

    Dimitri, Athena, Cassandra, and I went into Athens to attend our friend Nisette's art opening of her gorgeous marble sculptures, then went out for a long lubricous lunch. We ended the afternoon at a taverna in Kolonaki. Something in our conversation which I was too drunk to remember made Athena start to cry right at the table. It really upset Dimitri, so I went outside to retrieve her, and she was punching the side of the building. I finally got her calmed down. I'm pretty sure she was more than a little tipsy herself. Even though she is only sixteen, restaurants don't demand ID at all here in Greece, especially for the foreigners. We then checked into a nice hotel, The Athens Gate, located near Hadrian's Wall. We got two doubles, Dimitri and Cassandra in one room, and Athena and me in the other. We decided to catch the movie Shampoo, *but I was so inebriated, I couldn't keep from seeing double, not a great way to watch a movie, and in any case, I actually fell asleep (passed out more likely) before it was over.*

When we got back to the hotel, I was definitely not feeling well. I took a shower and lay down to try and nap. When I woke up, I still felt pretty awful, but some incredible out-of-the-blue stroke of will power got me up and dressed again, and we left at nine p.m. to meet Constantine at the Stagecoach Restaurant in Kolonaki.

Before meeting up at the Stagecoach, Athena and I went by Nisette's studio so she could join us. I felt a bit better until I drank an orange soda at the bar, and then it was all downhill. I can't remember ever being that sick! Dry heaves until five a.m.

It was a double-karma whammy: one, because I'd avoided remembering (and hence having to make a decision about) the fact that I was pregnant and, therefore, not able to go drinking all day with my usual impunity; and two, because I was actualizing licentious fantasies respecting the young and lovely body of the young and lovely and cooperative (and confused) Athena. One does not get off scot-free (no pun intended) from these things.

While I was kissing her right breast, Athena had said (though not really seriously), "Stop and look what you're doing. Why do you think you're any different than the others you keep warning me about?" It did make me stop and wonder afterward just what it was that made me feel superior. Yet, I did. It was something to do with being a believer, sensing something about the spiritual boundaries of sexual behavior which prevents

permanent harm. "The big kids and the little kids again." Just what was
going on anyway, God?

When I first rented the little house not far from George's (for
seventy-five dollars a month) from an American girl named Cathy who
was living on Hydra and taking care of a few absentee owners' homes, I
agreed to share it with an even younger girl from Oslo, Norway, named
Mette Jakobssen. She was just seventeen and had traveled all the way
from Oslo by herself. She was yet another friend of George's, and we
quickly discovered we had much in common and became friends. She
was an attractive and very charming girl—and I admit I developed a
little crush on her. And then something—not at all out of character on
Hydra—happened. She started seeing Jean Marc, who'd turned up again
like a bad penny. (Without the complication of Marianne being around,
he and I got along much better.) Mette loved to tease me, and one day
at Tasso's, after she'd left for the market, Jean Marc asked me if we were
sleeping together. I laughed (because though I wanted to, we weren't)
and said, "You missed something going on the last time, and now you
suspect it's going on again, but you're wrong."

Hydra is, and has always been, very incestuous. Sooner or later, it
seemed like everybody slept with everybody. So it goes.

Jean Marc and Mette began their affair soon afterward. Mette was quite
taken with Jean Marc, although she knew, of course, about his passion
for her rather-famous fellow Norwegian, Marianne. Some weeks into
their liaison, when she got the news that her father had suddenly died
of a heart attack, Mette needed to return immediately to Oslo but was
very distressed to have to go.

Though she wasn't very close to her father, a stern Norwegian
lawyer, she was a good daughter, so she packed and arranged to take the

early boat the next morning. I went down to the port with her, and I knew she was hoping Jean Marc would show up to say goodbye. But he didn't.

After the ferry left, I stayed at the café by the quay, drinking coffee and reading the *Herald Tribune*. Jean Marc showed up about an hour later.

"Is she gone?" he asked.

"She was so hoping to say goodbye to you," I remonstrated, shaking my head. "You couldn't get up an hour earlier?"

He smiled and sat down at the table. "I never said that I was brave," he answered, quoting the lyric from "So Long, Marianne":

You left when I told you I was curious,
I never said that I was brave*

We all did that from time to time: made references to the lyrics in some of Leonard's most familiar songs. The island was so defined for us by that great love affair shared by Leonard and Marianne—and by the music it inspired—it seemed only natural.

I chatted with Jean Marc for a while, then left to go back to the now-empty house and do some mundane chores. But when I came down for dinner, I heard that Jean Marc had taken the afternoon boat to Athens in search of Mette, to say a proper goodbye. He told me later that he did find her, and I was very happy for her that he'd made the effort. Jean Marc often played the cold-hearted cynic (not too difficult to pull off when one's a world-traveled Parisian) and always affected a very blasé, disinterested attitude. But like most of us on Hydra, he was a real sentimentalist at heart.

---

* "So Long, Marianne," Leonard Cohen

Our relationship morphed into a kind of love/hate teasing intimacy. Once, when he came to our house for dinner just before Mette left, he went over to the stove where I was making spaghetti sauce, tasted it, then added more salt without so much as a by-your-leave, something I would never have permitted anyone else to do.

Another time, I was there all alone and the door burst open at five a.m. Jean Marc rushed through the kitchen and into the bedroom where I was sleeping and blurted out, "I'm dying for a cigarette; do you have any?"

"Jean Marc," I said, barely awake, "I don't smoke."

"Damn," he muttered, and off he went again without so much as a "Sorry I woke you" or even "Good night, go back to sleep."

One of the last things Mette asked me before she departed so suddenly was whether I'd decided to try and visit Marianne in Oslo.

"Do come," she said. "If you don't stay with Marianne, you can stay at my family's house with me."

I told her I would only come if I heard from Marianne that she wanted to see me again.

December 15—Two more days to go before my departure.

I had a very bizarre dream last night, betraying an old familiar concern. I climbed a flight of rickety old stairs (staircases are a frequent theme in many of my dreams) and found T., whom I was apparently visiting, lying on a very rumpled, litter-type bed. His face was spattered with flecks of grey paint, and somehow, I already knew that my former philosophy professor and erstwhile rival for Rita's affections had taken up painting. He greeted me in his usual way, with relief and signs of pleasure, and we talked.

He said he had started working on a picture of a female form from memory and didn't realize until part way through that it was Rita. He seemed pleased that his memory recalled each line of her body in detail. He told me that she would be back soon and we could all have lunch together. I was surprised by this news, but I didn't show it. I had apparently come to console him for having lost her once again. I casually inquired what the status between them was now. He said, "She has not left me." He was very happy and relieved and, as usual, showed no awareness this news might distress me in any way.

I was very upset by this news but remained calm and placid. I asked him where his wife was, and he replied that she was off at a seminar at the University of Washington. He felt this would facilitate the separation from her he was determined, this time, to go through with. I told him of a conversation I'd had with Rita the year before in which she seemed to feel certain things had truly finished, and she'd asked me, "Don't you think so?" I'd replied, "No," and she'd confessed, "Sometimes, I don't either, but after so much time, it looks impossible." I told him I knew that, somehow, I was right about it not being over yet and tried to give the impression that I was happy at the confirmation of my intuition.

He told me it was now necessary for Rita to stay in NYC with John, his ex-best friend, but it was only a temporary arrangement. John had apparently been acting completely mad over the entire situation. Rita had told him she'd never loved him but always loved T. I wondered how she would justify another shift in her emotions and immediately envisioned the argument she would offer—something to do with the pragmatics of emotional life. I thought fleetingly that maybe for me, finally, this thing had ended, but I did not maintain or pursue that thought.

Somewhere around this time, I woke up.

That dream was followed by several days of the same kind: I am speaking with Rita. She tells me she has T.'s assurance that this year they are finally going to get together. She seems solicitous of my feelings about the matter, which seems incongruous to the present situation but which did not strike me this way in the dream. She asks me what I would like to do, and

I am aware, in facing Rita, of an overwhelming feeling of bone-shattering weariness—a sense of irretrievable, irreparable loss. This is so strong a sensation it almost makes me physically ill. And I reply that as our lives have taken us in very different directions anyway, I would like to finally be done with it and never see her again. I can't believe she has an expectation that we are all going to go through this frustrating triangular relationship yet again. The aching sense of sadness is unbearable. It feels like we are living a real-life version of Sartre's play, No Exit.*

The recalcitrance of my Taurean nature refuses, far beyond any logical calculation, to accept the inexorable movement of time and development. As I speak to her, I feel the feeble flame of connection flicker and go out, and I feel a part of me that I have nourished and cultivated way beyond its useful time engulfed with blackness and despair. I am left feeling embarrassed to have endured so much pain and frustration and to have accepted a suborned, secondary status for such a long time.

Dreams! Whew.

December 16, 1975

This is my last night in my house on Hydra. I cannot believe that tomorrow I will surrender the house to two young Greek guys that I've rented it to. I will meet the donkey man who will carry all my clothes and possessions down to the port, and I will take the walk down Donkey Shit Lane one last time. Then, I will board the two o'clock ferry and depart. It seems, in some ways, like five years since I arrived this time instead of just six months!

I recall like yesterday my concern, as I approached Hydra again after two years' absence, that I would faint from excitement and end up on the boat until it got to Spetses. I vividly remember arriving at the beginning of the summer and staying with Brandy, way up on the mountain in Palmer's house, then living two months with George in his big house before moving to my own little one. I think back on the scenes with Marilyn, with Skip, with Helga and Michel, and with Skip developing a crush on me, which I was keenly aware of but could not acknowledge, and Helga and her son Michel always arguing. All I could hear was her screaming at him, "Arrêt, Michel!" Many huge, magnificent, delicious dinners every night for ten or twelve people. The rocks and swimming every day at Montreal Beach! The gorgeous water dazzling, azure and clear, straight to the bottom fifteen feet below. And how we all laughed when the huge ferry boat would pass, way out in the channel, and we "regulars" would pick up our towels and books and bags and stand and wait for the wake that would come ten minutes later, swamping the towels of the "newbies." And dancing until four a.m. at Cavos. And reconnecting again, so briefly yet so beautifully, with Axel. The awful scene the night I took mescaline with him and the drunken maid's rant which precisely characterized the mess that Leonard had made by permitting Suzanne to move into his and Marianne's peaceful, lovely home. And George asking to talk with me and sitting on the rocks while he told me he was going to close up the house this year, so I would have to find another place to stay. Because, he said, Marilyn and her sister (who were also staying there) had scandalized the Greeks with all their parties and affairs, at least according to that old shrew Angeliki, his housekeeper! And then the plans with Marilyn to rent a house together when George and Skip departed for India and her excitement when she told me, "I've found a place!" And then, like the fickle woman she was, changing her mind at the last minute, two days after George and Skip had left, and deciding to follow them to India. And living in Lindsey's little house, which costs seventy-five dollars a month, and Mette deciding she would share it with me instead. And all the ambiguities of Mette, so young and yet so flirtatious! And the challenge, ostensibly removed when she became involved with Jean Marc. And Marilyn's friend Philip asking if he could stay awhile in the house as well, and his transformation, after Lindsey returned, from a shy and quiet *poet to a really effeminate gay, and his hesitant intimacy with Lindsey. And, of course, James and the morning-after jokes about how I might be pregnant. . . . "It occurs to me it wasn't exactly the best time of the month, ha ha." My friend (and would-be lover) Kathy's arrival with her gay friend Mick and the trips with them to Mykonos and Santorini. Kathy's anger at my indifference to her, so taken was I at the time with Mette. And the guilt and relief I felt after Kathy told me on Santorini that she was leaving to join a group of friends we'd run into while there. And Vivi and Vibe, ah, lovely Danish lesbians, and Jeff Brown and Marsha Picaud who lives in Athens but used to live with Richard Brautigan, the* Trout Fishing in America *author, and is on the cover of one of his books,* The Pill Versus the Spring Hill Mining Disaster. *Marsha, who thinks we are all, well, the magical ones, anyway, from another planet. Jeff Brown, Barbara Neogi's son, with his lovely, generous, placid voice and easygoing boyish surface and gentle demeanor with all the right combinations of intensity and sadness underneath. James again, and Mette's father's death, and all the departures, and pregnancy, and solitude. And peace and quiet in the joyful realization that I'm not going to freak out, and I like being alone (for the first time in my life).*

Rainy, cold, simple days interspersed with blazing sunsets and rainbows and homemade soups, neighborly dinners, the diminishing numbers and increasing affection of the foreign community. Turkey with all the fixing at Dimitri's beautiful studio on Thanksgiving and, later, Athena briefly in my bed. The perking of a red gas heater. The contentment of a clean kitchen. Then, finally, the conflict of the big decision: life or death, too hard to make. Vivi and Vibe tell me, "Come to Denmark. You can get an abortion there for free. Make up your mind when you have all the alternatives in front of you." And I resolve that I will go there and then make my decision. Please, God, I've always been on the side of life. I don't even kill bugs if I can scoop them up safely and dump them outside.

All finished now. Over; kaput. Not one-tenth the writing I intended to do, but, oh! What a life experience! It reminds me of Thoreau's epitaph that he wrote himself: "My life has been the poem I would have writ, but I could not both live and utter it."

Yet there is still the intention not to give up. I may find time in the morning, maybe something good in the wind. Please, please, please, let it be. And dare I risk requesting the bonus: Soon . . . bring me back to Hydra! Please, please, please.

When I eventually left Hydra that year, even after all the friends with whom I'd hung out (people I loved and admired) were gone, it was the island itself—its energy and atmosphere, the sheer beauty of the place—that caused me to depart with such a heavy sense of grief.

I knew it would be quite some time before I could return.

To this day, I remember how I walked to the back of the ferry with tears streaming down my face to watch the island in winter now—quiet, gray, and desolate—gradually disappear from view.

I received a postcard from Marianne:

Come and visit. Would love to see you again.

So, after spending six months on Hydra, the longest I'd ever stayed, I bought a student charter ticket and flew to Copenhagen to stay with the two young Danish lesbians, Vivi and Vibe, two blonde-haired, blue-eyed crazy beauties who had been renting a house high above the port on Hydra and living there along with the owner's son, Jeff Brown (who later won an Academy Award for his first short film, *Molly's Pilgrim*). I'd formed a little social group with them during the last two months I was there.

They'd departed Hydra two weeks before me, and the three of them hitchhiked to Copenhagen. When I arrived there, Jeff met me at the airport and escorted me to Christiana, the hippie squatters' section of the city.

Then we all spent Christmas at their farmhouse on an island.

I was three months pregnant by then and aware of the fact I had to make a definite decision about whether to have the baby or not. The girls had told me back on Hydra that abortion was free in Denmark, and I could get one there if that's what I decided. I'd spoken to Jean Marc about it before he left. He asked me one day when I was sitting in the port and looking, I guess, rather pensive.

He asked, "Do you have a problem?"

I answered, "Well, it's not a big problem right now, but it will become a progressively bigger problem as time goes by."

He was very perceptive, I'll give him that, and he instantly got the drift.

"Have it!" he said. "Go ahead—do it!"

And I remembered what Leonard had told me when discussing his own children: "The Roshi said, 'Go, have children, live your life!'"

I hesitated for a moment and then answered, tentatively, "I just might."

So here I was in Denmark, and the time to make a decision was at hand. I received a letter from James asking me not to go through with it, and I'd responded that I hadn't made up my mind but would not involve him in any way. I told him when I got back to the States, I wouldn't contact him, and he was free to either get in touch or not. (He did, but that's another story.)

Vivi and Vibe welcomed me like a long-lost relative, and Jeff took a bus out to meet me at the airport. At first, we stayed in a friend's squat in Christiania, a "free-occupied" part of old Copenhagen where a good portion of the gay community lives and where no one paid any rent. And then I had a very pleasant, simple country Christmas with my new friends on a Danish island called Mun, which means "moon." (Yep, Christmas on the moon!)

And there was a spot of blood in my underwear—perhaps this was a sign. I decided to wait and see if it got worse or went away.

Then it did go away . . . and I was somehow relieved.

The decision had been made.

I chose life.

Two days after Christmas, we all returned to Copenhagen where Vivi and Vibe were invited to a big after-Yule party. They took me along, of course—but was that ever a mistake on my part. I would've been much happier had I stayed at their comfy, warm flop. I did learn a valuable lesson, though, about being with heavy drinkers when you're not drinking. Vibe got so drunk that when we left the party at one a.m., taxi drivers took one look at the condition she was in and zoomed off without picking us up (it seems there is quite a bit of upchucking in taxis in Copenhagen).

After about half an hour of futilely trying to hail a cab in the freezing cold night, I was getting pretty frantic. Vibe was so out of it that when Vivi tried to get her to behave in front of prospective rides, Vibe bit her so hard through her thick winter coat, it drew blood. *Jesus, what have I got myself into*, I wondered.

Finally, I marched back up the stairs to the still throbbing party and berated everyone (in English, of course) about letting someone get that drunk, and I insisted that someone drive us home. Someone actually did after they all had a big laugh at this distraught, pregnant (sober) American. It's a night I'll never forget.

Oh, and did I mention that earlier in my visit, Vibe casually alluded to a job she'd had doing shows at a Copenhagen sex club with another lesbian, performing oral sex on one another for well-heeled Asian men?

"But that's when I was a heroin addict," she added, "so it really didn't bother me that much."

The next morning, I called Marianne and made arrangements to move on to Oslo, Norway. I booked a ticket on a huge ocean-going ferry, a beautiful, immaculate ship. I had my own little cabin for the overnight journey from Copenhagen to Oslo. The passage included dinner. It was a huge smorgasbord, but I was too seasick to partake of much of it. It sure looked good, though.

Marianne picked me up at the harbor, and I spent ten days with her and Axel. It's funny; maybe it was the pregnancy, or the very different locale, but there was very little magic attached to that visit and virtually no unrequited passion either. Our little *affaire du coeur* was, in the end, destined to remain just a lovely memory. We slept chastely (once again) in her big double bed. This time I was the reluctant partner. Oddly, when I was pregnant, I had absolutely no desire for sex.

We went for long walks in the city park and ate at home or in local restaurants. We went to the movies (*The Night Porter*) and spent New Year's Eve at the apartment of an American woman who was married to a Norwegian man. They had several children, but I don't remember them much. Initially, Mette, whom I'd also seen quite often, was supposed to accompany us, but at the last-minute, Marianne declared there was no room in the car, so she wasn't allowed to come (I think Marianne might have been a bit jealous over my obvious interest in Mette).

Axel and I hung out when Marianne went to work during the day as a secretary at a North Sea oil-producing company (hence, her frequent references in correspondence to "oil rigs" and saying "hallo between the oil rigs"). She did invite me to stay in Oslo and live with her and Axel and have the baby in Norway, but I was way too familiar with the vagaries of her moods and inclinations (La Donna È Mobile!) to even consider such a thing. And in fact, I never would have considered it, even if things between us had been different.

Who had changed, Marianne or me?

Both of us, utterly.

All moving things require a third principle. Hydra was our third principle. I didn't realize that until its absence. Without Hydra, I couldn't be compromised by Marianne. Without Hydra, I could not be touched. There was a sense of something incomparably beautiful, irreparably lost. There was no possibility that I imagined the original scenario. I recall it too well. But is there a possibility of imagining it happening again? Is there life after death? I'll keep the candle burning still. It is my role but no longer my primary one.

Marianne, where once I wept from the pain of your power, now I wept for the pain of its loss. Not even one tiny, sly smile of retribution there. The situation had passed beyond the baser instincts in the game. The tragedy transcendent permitted us more fully our better selves.

After Oslo, I didn't see Marianne again for many years, and though we tried to stay in touch, our letters became more and more sporadic and further and further apart until, after several years, they stopped completely. I visited Hydra many times and heard that she'd been there too, or was expected, but we didn't reunite until 2011, both of us much older and maybe a little wiser.

Who's to say?

3

1976

After a week and a half in Oslo, I booked a charter to London and stayed with my friends in Cambridge until the end of January.

Here are some entries from my journal during that time, in January of 1976:

January 10

Just had a really fine weekend in London with Susan, who I am staying with in Cambridge again. It was one of those times when all connections are made properly and all timing unfolds just right. First, I rang up a girl I met on Hydra through Brian and Valerie (coincidentally named Rita) and arranged to spend Saturday night at her place in London. Then I got tickets to the five-o'clock performance of Rosencrantz and Guildenstern Are Dead *at the Criterion Theater in Piccadilly, my first London stage play. It was excellent! Performed by the Young Vic Company. Then Susan and I went to SoHo and found a very nice, quiet little French restaurant for dinner. Later on, a bit of an adventure, it was off to Kensington to try and find a friend (ex-lover, of course) of Marianne's. She'd insisted that I look him up. He was a crazy Irish poet named Paul Desmond (yet another Hydra ex-pat, also friends with Anthony). I was told at Finch's, his local on Fulham Road, that he'd been barred for life! I couldn't get the barman to tell us what he'd done. It must have been something really horrendous, though, since his reputation for drunken atrocities was already well known there. I remembered that Brandy couldn't stand him. We tried another place they'd mentioned, The Queen's Elm, but to no avail. Two nice pints, though, and a decent way to end the evening.*

The next day, after a couple of drinks in a Younger's pub off Oxford Street, we ate lunch in an Indian restaurant, a very good one. I had a delicious (and very hot!) chicken vindaloo and then went on to the British Museum, which was packed with people coming to see a Turner watercolor exhibit. I've always liked Turner, especially his later stuff, and we were lucky to have gotten in on the last day of the show. Then we went to the movie Children of Paradise, *a fantastic film, finally seeing it to the end, and then had a quick drink at the Crown and Scepter pub with London Rita before catching the train back to Cambridge.*

I had tried getting in touch with Brandy and got further than I expected. I spoke to somebody who advised contacting John Anthony, who worked for Island Records and was expecting to hear from Brandy. I also tried to ring Nick Broomfield (another of Marianne's exes) but with no success.

For a brief moment, yesterday, while walking out of New Oxford Street in the rain and clouds, I experienced one of those flashes of disorientation (nonspecific anxiety, though not too intense) which makes all the surrounding buildings and structures loom up overhead and seem foreign and vaguely hostile. It was luckily very fleeting but still something I chose to put immediately out of my head. I wouldn't ever want to go through that again, but it reminded me that once you've gone through the prelude to madness, it's never completely eradicated. Maybe it was because the movie I was on my way to see, I had first seen with Rita in Los Angeles. But it was another time and another movie with Rita when I first felt that panic, so strong that time, and so new and overwhelming a sensation. I quietly patted my knee

Oslo January 14th 1976

Dearest Judith

We miss you.

Hope all went well after you left us at the airport.

Had a letter from Jane today and she is still pregnant
9 weeks. Christina either lost it or wasent pregnant at
all. Anyway Jane is realy happy about it, and she told
me how I can get pregnant to, just using her method.
I will have to tell you about another time, this is
just hallo between oil-rigs.

Cold as hell up here, I mostly sleep, no more beer for
me I put on a couple of kilos already. Mette is leaving
tomorrow I will see her tonight for a while. She is such
a beautiful little creature.

Have a feeling Leonard is coming this way sometime in
February, cannot wait to see him. We may together get
Axel settled for next year too.

Back to the old "oil-rigs". All good things from Axel.

Love Marianne

lo from Valerie and Brian, I just had a card from them.

Figure 4.

to comfort myself, to keep from screaming. I think I really just needed to get home and face the apprehensions I was feeling and adjust to however good or bad it was going to be. It's the terror of being dependent on others that I had to dispel. That situation, I must at all costs avoid.

Today brought a letter from Marianne [see fig. 4], brief but pleasantly unexpected. Jane is still pregnant. I cross my fingers for her. Christina is not. And she had a card and greetings for me from Brian and Valerie. She also mentioned that she feels Leonard might appear anytime now in Oslo. While I was there, I had the same intuition. Today, I will send a birthday card to Axel. Marianne says of Mette, "She is such a beautiful little creature. I will see her for a while this evening."

Another journal entry:

January 24

Another cold, windy day at "The House" in Cambridge. I sit huddled in front of the electric fire unable to summon the energy for more than one brief shopping trip. In stores, I'm bothered frequently by headaches, no doubt because of the combination of the faulty heating methods here and my chronic sinus blockage (how dull). I can't wait to get home but dread the trip back to Brussels. Why can't I remember what it was like to drink as often as I did? Now I just crave ice cream, hot fudge, bananas, and wet walnuts. I don't think I'll ever seriously go back to drinking. But how will I ever relate to my friends, dipsomaniacs all, when in a state of carefully chosen perpetual sobriety?

It amazed me to discover that anyone might have thought me an alcoholic. I have not even considered any serious drinking for such a long time. Even on Thanksgiving, when everyone else got drunk, I finally settled for an eggnog and one glass of white wine with dinner. Of course, I always knew my drinking was no more than a habit, though admittedly a compelling and, at times, expensive one. But it surprises me now to recall the skeptical glances of my friends when I presented it that way.

Sometime earlier, both Rita and John Taurek (the semi-famous philosophy professor) had asked me why I didn't believe I was an alcoholic since I was pretty much a daily drinker. I thought about it for a while, and then I said, "Because, if you were describing me to someone who didn't know me, you would not say, 'She's very bright and articulate and has a great personality, but she is an alcoholic.'" And they both thought about it for a moment, and then agreed. "You're right," they said. "We would not describe you that way."

At the end of January, I returned to New Jersey.

Just before I left Norway, I called my mother on the phone. I figured I'd better prepare her for the news. I was not surprised by her reception.

"You have ruined what should be the happiest moment of my life!" she said.

Well, that was to be expected. My mother, as wonderful a woman as she was—strong, and engaging, intelligent, and blessed with a wonderful sense of humor and an unerring sense of style—was probably the one person I knew who was the most concerned about what others thought of her. She was very proud and very competitive, and any perceived fault or criticism in any area of her life, whether it be her reputation, children, home—pretty much anything that involved her—was NOT to be tolerated.

My mother came from a very large, very conservative Irish-Catholic family. She had five brothers and many nieces, nephews, aunts, uncles, and cousins, and we were all very close-knit. I think she only adjusted to the fact that I was expecting a baby after Torie was born. She declared we would have no baby shower, that we would handle all the costs for the birth and infancy ourselves. And she was as good as her word on that score. She paid all my hospital and doctor expenses, and since I had to have an unscheduled caesarian (Torie was breech), it amounted to a fair amount of money.

It was a period of understandable anxiety in my life. The mood swings of pregnancy, with no partner (male or female) to lend support, took a toll. I shared an apartment with my sister, Cindy, in New Milford, New Jersey. I was very lucky, though, to get my old job at the lab back. Everyone there was terrific to me.

I worked until I was eight months pregnant, then went on disability unemployment. And after Torie was born, I remained on unemployment for ten months, and my supervisors at the lab did me the supreme kindness of reassuring the Unemployment Office that they intended to rehire me, so I was not even required to look for other work. That provided me with enough money to pay my share of the rent on the apartment and take care of all Torie's doctor bills and my day-to-day expenses. I was even able to save enough (after selling my Volkswagen Beetle) to move us back to Los Angeles.

Card to Marianne, with the inside text transcribed (see fig. 5)

5 March 1976

Dear Marianne,

Saw this card and couldn't help thinking of you; "Chelsea Hotel" just played on the radio and I knew it was time to write. Hope the Norwegian winter has not got you down and out, here the weather has been mild lately—promise of an early spring.

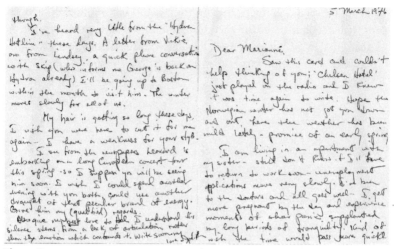

Figure 5.

I'm living in an apartment with my sister—still don't know if I'll have to return to work soon—unemployment applications move very slowly. I've been to the doctor's and all goes well—I get more pregnant by the day and experience moments of sheer panic supplanted by long periods of tranquility. Kind of wish the time would pass more quickly though.

I've heard very little from the "Hydra Hotline" these days. A letter from Vickie, one from Lindsey, a quick phone conversation with Skip (who informs me George is back on Hydra already). I'll be going up to Boston within the month to visit him. The winter moves slowly for all of us.

My hair is getting so long these days. I wish you were here to cut it for me again—I have a weakness for your style. I see from the newspapers Leonard is embarking on a long European concert tour this spring so I suppose you will be seeing him soon. I wish I could spend another evening with you both, could use another draught of that peculiar brand of energy. Give him my (qualified) regards. Also give my best love to Axel. I understand his silence stems from a lack of articulation rather than the emotion which confounds it. Write soon my love.

Judith

Several weeks later, Marianne wrote me back (see fig. 6).
     Here are a pair of journal entries from that time:

March 5

I am incredibly pregnant now. I spoke to Rita on the phone last night and finally mentioned my feelings of nausea and loathing attached to the alteration of my physical condition. I think it has something to do with the loss of body image and the realization that my situation is never going to be the same. I have always abjured all roles, titles, definitions in order to preserve my individuality, but I am now about to take on the biggest, most committed, and oldest role in the world. I'm about to become just another mother! Where can all this endless self-scrutiny end? While meaning should be multiplying and confirming, something is gradually slipping further and further away from me.

*   And this might just be a manifestation of the predictable five-month antepartum depression. How disgusting!*

March 11

There is a thing living inside me, something I know very little about. It thumps against my insides. I cannot predict when that's going to happen. It

Oslo, 29th March 1976

Dearest Judith & Co.,

Lots of thoghts to you all the time, find it so difficult
to write long letters, I somehow hate that kind of contact
want to see you and be with you.

Axel and I are working harder than ever, we want to get this
examn this summer at all cost. He is defenetly leaving town
this next season. First we are working till middle of July
then I hope to get a house for a month on Hydra. And then
he leaves for Canada or the States. What I will do is still
in the air. Have to keep on making money to help Axel and
to keep alive. I don't have to stay in Norway, but have come
up with no better solution yet. Time will show.

Are you heading this way in the summer? when I know if I get
a house or not I will let you know. When is baby due?

Hope things are well, did you get a job? I hope you got
some sosial security instead.

Spring is in the air, leaving for the little country house
for Easter, Axel reads well down there. Cant wait to get out
of this town. Steve is gone, I just ended up dead, and told
him no hope, but hell it took so long. I feel I can breath
again. Back to the oil rigs. Keep in touch, next time near a
phone you don't have to pay for phone us.

Love Marianne

P.S.   Phone 11.30.46
_____

When you see Jeff ask him to send
all possible brochures on studies
in the States to Axel. -M-

Figure 6.

seems to prefer me in motion and protests my inactivity by kicking me. Can it prefer? Protest? Anything? I wish the baby was here now, so I could touch it and start knowing it. I finally believe in its existence and its relationship to me. It already needs my blood, and I worry that it is not thick enough, but I don't take the daily prescribed tablets. I can't believe my body is not enough on its own.

Later, this baby will exist in a different relation to me—I will be the mother. Now I am just the carrier. I somehow provide it life. What kind of imposition is this? I worry that it won't recognize me, won't know that I'm the mother, will choose some other. What identifies me in this role? What if it looks at me someday and says, "You're not my mother!" It's like the feeling I used to get, standing in front of a classroom of kids when I was a substitute teacher. What if one of them realizes I'm not really a teacher? What makes them all believe I am? What if they just refuse to do what I say? What makes me their teacher?

Today is Rita's birthday; she's 28. We met when she was 22 and I was 24. Happy birthday, Rita.

It was during this time that I spent many hours listening to Leonard's iconic album, *New Skin for the Old Ceremony*. They're all iconic, I suppose, in their own way, but NSFTOC created quite a stir when it came out a couple of years earlier—most notably for the song "Chelsea Hotel #2," his thinly-disguised ode to Janis Joplin.

When I was visiting with Marianne in Oslo, she said, "Leonard used some of your poetry in one of his songs, didn't he?"

I was a little surprised that she was aware of that and kind of brushed it off.

"Yeah, I think something I sent him may have inspired a line or two."

I always suspected that his lovely song, "Take This Longing"—
which contained the lyric: "Everything depends upon on how close
you sleep to me"*—just might have been partly inspired by my poem.
Marianne apparently knew of it.

I'd been hoping a face-to-face meeting with Marianne could repair
whatever damage that poem had done to our relationship. I can't pretend there wasn't some bitterness in my motivation to write the poem,
then send it to Leonard, but I also wanted him to know that nothing
had happened the night he left us to be together—that she still cared
enough to respect the history they and that house and bedroom and bed
had shared.

And why did I think he showed the poem to her?

Well, I have a theory about that as well: I think he wanted her to
know he wasn't the only lover who ever betrayed her.

Here's another journal entry:

April 1976

*I am very pregnant now and thinking of Greece and Marianne as if it were
all just a lovely extended dream, long ago and far away. Leonard's new
album came out. The song he was working on that he taught me to sing
back in 1973 was on it, though very much changed, evolved, and much
more complicated, which was just as he had described his writing/compos-
ing process. It's still called "The Singer Must Die," though, and it inspired
me to write another poem to Marianne, mimicking the same rhythms and
cadences as the lyrics of that song.*

---

* "Take This Longing," Leonard Cohen

Insert to a birthday card to Marianne, transcribed (see figs. 7a–7b)

May 18, 1976

M.,

I have heard nothing from Jeff for several months, guess he is busy with school which closes soon, and I have been rather busy myself. If Axel is thinking of finishing his final high school year in N.Y.C. I think we could arrange it without too much difficulty, I could accompany him to registration and he could remain here until facilities in the city were located—but it is a bit far here for daily commuting. Can't estimate what expenses would be however Jeff would be helpful there, and I will try to contact him again. Some contribution from Leonard would probably be necessary (and not inappropriate!).

I was rather dismayed to hear Suzanne is back on Hydra already—if you don't make some arrangement to reclaim that house for your vacation this summer (at least!) you are a consummate fool! It cannot but risk some permanent damage if chaos is its only inhabitant. Brandy visited me some weeks ago while I was miserably ill with the flu, we had a good talk. The same school arrangement could be made for Axel in Montreal, he could help. If he's thinking of going directly to the university, information for overseas students' enrollment can be obtained from any university admissions office. For N.Y.U., write to:

Office of Admissions
New York University
NYC, NY USA

M.,

March 1976
~~April~~
May 18.

I have heard nothing from
Jeff for several months, guess
he is busy with school which
closes soon, and I have been
rather busy myself. If Axel is
thinking of finishing his final high
school year in N.Y.C., I think we
could arrange it without too much
difficulty, I could accompany him to
registration, and he could remain
here until facilities in the city
were located - it is a bit far
here for daily commuting. Can't
estimate what expenses would be however - Jeff would be helpful there, and
I will try to contact him again -
some contribution from Leonard would
probably be necessary (and not inappropriate!) I was rather dismayed to hear
Suzanne is back on Hydra already - if
you don't make some arrangement to
reclaim that house for your va-

Figure 7a.

(at least!)

cation this summer, you are a
consummate fool! It cannot but risk
some permanent damage, if chaos is
its only inhabitant.

Brody visited me some weeks
ago, while I was miserably ill with
the flu, we had a good talk. The
same school arrangements could be made
for Axel in Montreal, he could help.
If he's thinking of going directly to
the University, information for overseas
students enrollment can be obtained from
any University admission office.
e.g.: for N.Y.U. write to: Office of Admissions
                           New York Univ.
                           n.y.c. N.Y.
                           USA.

No news from Hydra, a post card from
Beatrice informs me the Geneva contingent
will take up residence there again this
summer — how I shall miss it! The
pregnancy proceeds on schedule and time
grows short (1st of July), no news from
Motti, did Jean Marc ever show up? à S.
write soon of plans — be well love Judith

Figure 7b.

No news from Hydra, a postcard from Beatrice informs me the Geneva contingent will take up residence there again this summer—how I shall miss it! The pregnancy proceeds on schedule and time grows short (1st of July), no news from Mette, did Jean Marc ever show up?

Write soon of plans—
be well A. G. T.

Love
Judith

In the journal entry, I still (mistakenly) referred to the song by its original title, "The Singer Must Die." On NSFTOC, Leonard has modified it slightly to "A Singer Must Die." Also from that same journal entry, a poem I wrote for Marianne:

For M.

If you ever remember the time that we met
You'll be forced to recall what you'd rather forget
Faith has been broken and time will not yield
Back to lovers of mirrors, the mysteries sealed
In their flesh
So, come to the window or come to the door
You have no excuse to refuse anymore
Time has been waiting, that you thought you'd all spent
And the man with the ledger appears for the rent
Of your gown.
Yet there's still potential in the clouds of the night
We'll repeat the key phrase 'til we all get it right
The man on the mountain adds up win and loss

And you find thirty pieces can ride on one toss
Of the dice.
Still you earned a title that outstrips the rest
As your soul picks the forms that your mind couldn't guess
The man in the moon, who's run out of rhyme
Comes to whisper "so long" for the very last time
In this game.

—Judy Scott, 1976

Victoria (Torie) Mary Scott was born on July 13, 1976, at Englewood Hospital in Bergen County, New Jersey.

It was a pretty gruesome delivery. She was breech, and they had to perform an unscheduled C-section. Nine hours of transition labor . . . I've never experienced such excruciating pain. But like all blessed events, I guess, in the end, it was more than worth it.

When Torie was six months old, my sister Cindy experienced a very traumatic relationship break-up, which actually involved some serious physical threats. Besides my unemployment, I'd been receiving my father's social security checks, and we got a lump sum for the time he spent in the VA Hospital, so I used it to take my sister and Torie on a trip to Hydra.

Torie and I stayed for two months, but my sister's ex contacted her, expressed enormous regret, and begged her to return, and after one month, she did. They were married the next year. Outside of that lovely excursion, and another wonderful Thanksgiving party at Dimitri Gassoumis' house, it was a quiet and rather lonely time for me. Getting accustomed to having exclusive responsibility for another being, especially a helpless baby, is never as easy in practice as one might imagine in theory. But I never regretted my decision, and Victoria Mary Scott was

Tuesday September 6th

Dearest little mother,

At last a letter from you, both my last letters came in
return, I have them at home will send them if you don't
believe me. Had no idear how you where, Victoria I love
that name. Could not tell you about your kind of birth,
I did not have it that way. You both look great, I am
so happy. Even Mette sent you a small present, if she
sent it to the same adress as I you probably did not
get that either. We talked about you every day around the
birth. We where in Hydra at the time. Spent a whole month
there with Mette and Axel. Rented a small house in Kamini
and had a summer of my life. Everything was nice, good
vibrations and love everywhere. Axel and Mette is still
there, Axel on his way to India in a couple of weeks.

Mette will probably stay the winter, I don't know for sure.
Strange to be back in Oslo and at work again. A bit sad
living without Axel, but I will get used to it.
As I sad Hydra was very beautiful this time around.
Saw Leonard again had some sweet times with him. George
was drinking a lot, but still the same old smile. Suzanne
somehow avoided me. Maggi was there she is a blessed one too.
Met a nice man older than me for a change, spent some dreamy
nights with him. Kamini kept us home a lot, did not go to
port that often. Parties I avoided, but Bill's Bar was a
nice place to drop in at all hours of the night or day.
Some poetryreading in the Miranda hotel, a few plays too,
so we had our portion of culture. Sinclair Lewis was there
Old George Slater and more. About Leonard and Suzanne I only
know that Leonard will stay on if he can get into a book or
something.   I do hope he can. He locked a bit sad but I
gather that is him anyway.

Coming home I fell into the arms of a very nice man, tender
as hell, cannot quite believe it for a norwegian. Anyway I
am playing it cool, so far so good. No plans of anything.

Meeting Julie next weekend, and will go with her to Stockholm
she is singing all over Europe. Travelling around Norway a
few days in a couple of weeks to be introduced to the "oil-
world" a bit of change from the usual officework. I will stay
on till Axel is getting it together. As a matter of fact I
could not live without doing something. Taking classes in
Japaneese and all that goes with it, gymnasticks twice a week
swimming etc. I keep it up. Had a great dream the other day
and have desided to start writing a book. A few pages every
afternoon. Already got a typewriter. Hope I will keep it up.

Would love to see you both. I might spend another month in
Hydra next Summer who knows. First the winter to get through.
Hope this reaches you. Miss you a lot and think of you often.
Keep well, kisses for Victoria and to you.

The adress I got your   Love Marianne
letter in return:
30 Rutland Ave.
Kearny N.J. 07032

Figure 8.

and still is the light of my life. A couple of months later, another letter from Marianne arrived (see fig. 8).

This time, I did phone my friend George to see if it was okay to come for a visit, and initially, he said we could stay with him until he was admonished by his housekeeper Angeliki (still the neighborhood scold) that if I arrived with a baby a year after staying with him, it would scandalize the entire local Greek community (yet again).

George found us a very nice house up Kalo Pigadi to stay in, a house owned by a woman named Eva Kellogg who'd been married to one of the heirs of the Kellogg's Corn Flake fortune. An American girl named Gwen, whom I knew from past years on Hydra, was the caretaker for the house (as well as for several others owned by wealthy foreigners). It was a lovely, authentic Greek house with a huge kitchen, living room, three bedrooms, and a beautiful terrace overlooking the island. The price for staying there was simply to buy fresh fish daily and feed their seven cats.

To my delight, Mette was back on Hydra again staying in Helen Marden's house not far from George's. My sister had to leave the island sooner than I did, so Mette watched Torie overnight for me when I took Cindy into Athens to catch her plane.

An interesting and wholly-Hydra moment happened on the boat when I was returning to the island. I struck up a conversation with a young American couple, Craig and Sharon, sitting at the table next to mine in the bar/restaurant inside the ferry. There was some beer imbibing involved. Anyway, they told me they were on a brief vacation from Craig's international residency in pediatrics.

They'd spent three months in Athens where he'd worked at a maternity hospital and were on their way to London to spend another three months following their one-week break. They'd decided to visit

Spetsi, the next island west of Hydra. I waxed eloquent on the far superior experience they'd find on Hydra and even invited them to stay at the Kellogg house with me.

They looked a little like I might be a touch crazy at that spontaneous invitation. But I was not able to persuade them to get off the boat with me, and they waved goodbye from the rail as they continued on to Spetsi.

I was more than a little surprised the next afternoon to see them sitting at a café on the port. I welcomed them warmly.

"What made you change your mind?" I asked.

"Well, you were right," they said. "Spetsi was rather boring and not nearly as scenic and beautiful as the brief view we got of Hydra, so we took the morning boat back here."

They'd booked into one of the quayside pensions, so I invited them to come up to the house the next day for lunch. They eagerly accepted, and Craig offered to give Torie a brief wellness exam when they came. I made tuna salad and Greek salad and had fresh bread and cheese and fresh fruit, which I served with wine and beer. We had a very nice meal on the terrace and, afterward, I'd see them in the port over the next few days. On their last evening, I joined them for dinner at Douskos Taverna and wished them bon voyage.

So . . . I was even more startled to see Sharon two days later sitting at a table in the port with a strange man, someone I didn't know.

"Holy crow!" I exclaimed (a favorite expression of mine—my variant of the overused, clichéd "Holy cow"). "What are you doing still here?"

"Oh, my holy Jesus," she replied. "I really need to talk to you! You know how you told us over lunch about the legend on Hydra that if a couple could stay together while here, they'd probably make it for the

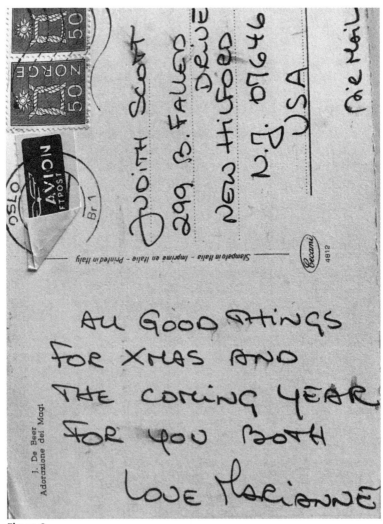

Figure 9.

rest of their lives? Well, I thought long and hard about that and, also, I'd met this lovely French artist who offered to let me stay with him for the winter, so I told Craig to go on by himself and he could give our parents whatever explanation he wanted. I was so tired of schedules and having to do all the household stuff by myself and having to constantly conform to his medical school needs. I just decided that wasn't the life I wanted, so I'm staying here for the winter with Pierre."

I had to laugh at that and couldn't help thinking to myself, *If I'd only kept my mouth shut about how magical Hydra is, Craig and Sharon might be happily ensconced in London by now.*

Then again, perhaps I merely accelerated the inevitable?

She seemed happy.

C'est la vie.

Back in New Jersey later that year, a Christmas postcard from Marianne found me (see fig. 9). She'd sent it to my old address. I was a new mother, full of happiness over my daughter—but also sad not to be back on Hydra, where my heart was always happy.

"All Good Things"—Marianne's signature sign-off.

I use it to this day.

4

1977 AND 1978

I received a letter from Marianne, dated March 15, 1977 (see fig. 10).

Card to Marianne, date April 23, 1977, transcribed

23 April 1977

Dear Marianne,

I saw this card in New Hope, Pennsylvania, and it reminded me of you: the beautiful, blonde bride, the embryo emerging after such a long gestation, the sharp claws of memory, and so much more. I was so glad to receive your letter, gladder still for your news. "Hierete" is such a lovely Greek word.

George told me it means "rejoice" and that's just how I feel, so glad for you, so pleased (there is hope for all of us yet and without compromises). I send greetings to your fiancée, I'm sure he must be very special (sure also that he must realize that you are). I only wish you could honeymoon in L.A. So how was Hydra? Beautiful, I'll bet—peaceful and emerging from the dismal winter—not yet sullied by the crowd—tell me all about your time there—how is the house? How is the brat doing? She knows her silence bugs me—so she doesn't write!—hope you both had a great time. I talked to Barbara Neogi on the phone last week—she said to send

In my office 15.3.77.

Dearest Judith

Long time no hear. On this end all is good. Mette is back
in Norway working away at the Theater. We are leaving for
Hydra for 10 days in April. Doing a cracy trip, but Mette
has to finish the work on Helens house and I need some sun.
Leonard phoned me the other day, the house is mine for that
week thank God. I am realy looking forward to this trip even
though it is short. Axel is well in India, returning some ,
time after Easter. Can't wait to see him again.

Winter long but thank God lots of snow. These days nothing
but grey, and wet and a bit of spring in the air. Worth
living again. Lots of things happening in my life. Fell in
love the real way middle of October, it's just growing day
by day. Havent felt like this since I met Leonard 17 years
ago. Too good to be true. He is still not divorced, have
three beautiful girls of 17 - 13 - and 12. Axel has already
met them years ago when he lived at my mothers house, they
were neighbours. He is my age tall dark and handsome with
curly hair. They are four brothers two of them I have known
for years. The world is small. Anyway we finally met one wet
Autumn day and have been together since. He just got himself
a beautiful apartment near the park, and I will slowly move
in. Trying to wait till divorce is over, I think I will feel
a bit better then. I have loved every minute with him so
far. He is going to the mountains with his daughters for
Easter, but I feel Hydra is calling me, because I am not
planning another summer there. Too many people to hot and
cracy. Will probably take our "honymoon" there sometime this
Autumn. Yes, We may even get married. I was pregnant with
him after one week, I who have not been able to get pregnant
for about 6 years. Anyway, timing was wrong I desided to wait.
Sometimes I regret, but I feel we have enough with 4 children
at the moment.

I heard about Naton Dunbar and Helen, how she ever left good
old Brice- I never understood. New Year's Eve sounded fun.
The one in Norway was fatal as far as I can remember. I remember
you sitting in the sofa wearing my black velvet jacket. And that's
it. Victoria Looks beautiful, such beautiful eyes. You are
heading for California you lucky one, I would love to spend
some time there, but my travelling is over for some time.
We are planning to build on my house in Larkollen, Jan has a
big boat and we might try to get hold of an old farm somewhere
in the mountains. Plans many plans I must admit I live from
day to day who knows to much about "tomorrow". I leave the
planning to him. He reminds me in many ways of Leonard.
There is something in him so tender, kind and genereous a rear
thing for a norwegian. We have already been in Spain for 10 days
just before Xmas. Fantastic trip, but Spain is not for me.
Work is calling, good to hear from Judith. Please keep in touch.
Who knows we may be in California too one day. One never knows.
All good things to you both.

                    love Marianne

Fig. 10.

her best—will spend the month of July on Hydra, asked for Axel (is he well?). Heard Leonard was in Montreal with dying mother. Do you have his L.A. address? I might drop in, don't know—mixed feelings there—reservations. Picking up everything and leaving makes me so uneasy but I must get out of here. The I Ching says all will go well—keep the faith, etc. It's so different with a baby—but of course you know that. She is fine, by the way, bigger brighter more beautiful, a pure joy.

Talked to Vicki who was trying to reach you (just to say hi) nothing else new.

I'm feeling kind of sentimental tonight, as I always do when writing to someone far way—I envy you in a clear positive way—to achieve something good, worthwhile after such a long hiatus. You have broken through, and I'm very proud of that, it renews my faith (that's what friends are for I think, to restore our faith). Can you see my smile? I can't let myself get too serious!

So, send me your news, send me your plans, send me what you have for me, I send you my

Love,
Judith

After a few months back in New Jersey, I was ready for change. I relocated back to Los Angeles when Torie was eleven months old in June of 1977. I sublet a one-bedroom apartment in Santa Monica that Rita had been renting (when she moved back in with John, who'd just returned from New York), and I stayed there for six months feeling dreadfully lonely and isolated.

I'd found a job right away and was once again working in a clinical lab, knowing in my heart and soul it was absolutely not what I wanted to be doing with my life but also knowing I could make the most money at something I had real experience in, and I was determined to support Torie and myself without seeking anyone else's help.

I kept in touch with many of my Hydra friends by snail mail in those days, but one evening, the phone rang. When I picked it up, a very familiar voice started laughing and, without introduction, sang into the receiver, "Oh, Danny Boy!"

"Anthony! Oh my god! Where are you? How'd you get my number?"

"I'm at Leonard's house in Brentwood," he said. "He sent me a ticket to come for a visit."

Sometime after Suzanne had moved the kids to France, she and Leonard attempted a reconciliation and rented a house in the Brentwood section of LA together.

"When can I see you?" I asked.

"Well, we're leaving for San Francisco tomorrow to stay with George Slater. Can you come up there?"

But I couldn't join them because of my responsibilities as a working single parent. I knew I wouldn't be able to get time off from a job I'd just started, so we just had a nice chat. Before we hung up, though, Anthony asked me to do him a favor. Suzanne was feeling miserably lonely, he said. Would I call her and arrange a get-together?

I'd last seen Suzanne on Hydra the previous fall. She was about to leave on the hydrofoil with Adam and Lorca and a new au pair, bound again to spend the winter in France. She came over to where I was sitting at a quayside café with my daughter next to me in an umbrella stroller. Suzanne bent down to look at Torie, who was then six months old.

"You decided to go through with it?" she asked.

"Yes," I replied, "and I'm very glad I did."

"Of course," she said in that same breathy angelic voice, "your children are your life."

Hmm, I thought, *that's a far cry from where she was about motherhood the year before.* Whatever . . .

I had no burning desire to see Suzanne ever again, but since Anthony had asked, I said, "Sure."

And so I did. I arranged lunch at the Bicycle Café on Wilshire Boulevard, in West Los Angeles, just a little south of where she and Leonard were living in Brentwood and also close to where I was working. We agreed to meet on my noon break the following week. I arrived at the appointed time and waited and waited . . . but no Suzanne.

Finally, I told the waitress I needed to order, having wasted half my lunch hour. Then Suzanne showed up—forty-five minutes late—and with her new au pair in tow.

"Who's watching the kids?" was the first thing I asked.

"Oh," she replied, "the maid will mind them until we get back. Do you know where I can buy some drugs?"

I told her I had no idea. "I'm working full-time now and taking care of my baby. I have no time for drugs. I don't do them anymore."

After that brief opening sally, Suzanne was decidedly less interested in our encounter and, after a few desultory comments about Anthony, Leonard, and some others we knew in common, there was a distinct lull in conversation.

Finally, I told her I had to get back to work and left. We made no other plans to meet and, though I heard of her whereabouts and activities through the Hydra pipeline, it was a long time before I saw her again.

But I do remember thinking, after knowing both Marianne and Suzanne: *Oh Leonard, why did you have to go to such extremes to prove to Marianne you could live with someone her polar opposite?*

I honestly don't know if that was true. Certainly, it's an oversimplification, but it struck me that way over and over again.

Then, by chance, I saw an advert in the UCLA student newspaper for a house to share with another single mother. We met several times to see if we could get along, and I moved in with her and her four-year-old son, Adam, in November of 1977.

Torie was then fifteen months old. Sadly, my new roommate, Dolly, turned out to be a horror show, a classic passive-aggressive and very angry lady with a pretty awful family history.

Dolly's father was the number-two man in the Mississippi Ku Klux Klan and a terrible, sadistic tyrant, and her mother had up and left the family of six kids when Dolly was ten years old. That was after their house had burned down, killing her twin brothers, because their father had figured out a way to steal electricity by putting pennies on the electric meter, which shorted out the system.

You can't make this stuff up.

I cooked dinner every day for Adam, Torie, and me as Dolly subsisted on brown rice and boiled vegetables. The good news was that she decided to move to San Diego a year after I moved in—and I got the house! It was a beautiful old farmhouse in a great location on the west side of Culver City, and I live there to this day, now as the co-owner with Monika (of course).

In 1978, I went on the TV show *Jeopardy* as a contestant and came in second, back when you got to keep whatever money you won (that $1,300.00 came in very handy).

I stayed at the clinical lab for about two years, then did a whole variety of different things to support us: I worked for a non-union film-extras agency, helping to coordinate large groups of extras and sometimes being one myself; after that, I got a job through a friend at a publishing company—Price Stern Sloan—in the art department. As a result of that, I have the proud honor of having type-set *Murphy's Law* by Arthur Bloch. I became an itinerant typesetter for several years and worked in many different print shops and design studios, doing photo-typesetting and developing photos in the darkroom. It was definitely much more interesting than the clinical lab, if still not really what I wanted to do.

When Torie was four, and before I got together with Monika, I started taking acting lessons with Milton Katselas, a very well-known acting coach (who just happened to be Greek). He also happened to be a Scientologist, and all the students in his classes were required to sign a contract not to drink or smoke anything intoxicating for twenty-four hours prior to each class (an agreement I regularly broke).

There were several students in our group who later became quite famous. My favorites were Patrick Swayze and his wife, Lisa Niemi. We became good friends and would go out after our lessons (which were held every Tuesday and Thursday from eight to midnight at the Attic Theater on Sunset Boulevard in Hollywood) to Cantor's Deli or Theodore's or Café Figaro in West Hollywood and talk endlessly about the business, the craft, and the art of acting.

A group of us would get together at house parties as well, and Patrick taught Torie how to do the Texas two-step when she was four. I attended those classes for about two years. I loved them and did really well, too, but the price of tuition kept going up, and I had to drop out when I couldn't afford it anymore. Still, I cherish those memories.

Many years later, I ran into Patrick and Lisa at an IFC party, after the Spirit Awards, on the beach in Santa Monica. "You look good, Judy," he said to me.

"So do you, Buddy," I replied. (All his friends called Patrick "Buddy." It was his family nickname.) He was *so* talented—the best actor in the class—and such a sweet, friendly man. I was just heartbroken when he passed away from pancreatic cancer a few years ago, at fifty-seven, way too young and way too sad. So life went on, but all the while, I was trying like crazy to save enough money to return to my beloved Hydra.

It wouldn't be until May of 1982, when Torie was six, that I had the wherewithal to take off for a month.

5

1980S AND BEYOND

In 1982, after a six-year absence, I returned to Hydra at last, bringing six-year-old Torie with me. I had lost track of Marianne for a time but fervently hoped I might find her once again on Hydra. So it was particularly disappointing to be informed when I arrived that she'd been there and departed only two weeks before our arrival. I'd brought two T-shirts from Venice Beach with me, hoping to give them to her and Axel. When I returned home to Los Angeles that year, I left them (and a note) with our mutual friend Maggie Martin to be delivered to Marianne when she next visited. She did return two years later and received my gift finally and sent me a lovely thank-you note (which I no longer have). My letter to Marianne, dated February 3, 1984, is the last of our written correspondence that has been preserved (see fig. 11).

I arranged (again through friends) to rent a small cottage owned by a German named Hartmut Porsche. It was high up, off Donkey Shit Lane, and quite close to George's house. It wasn't very big but had everything I needed: good-sized open living/dining/kitchen and a small bathroom on the main floor and two single twin beds on the second floor. It had a small terrace, as well, but no view. The price was right, though, and everything was clean and attractive.

The property where Bill Cunliffe had moved his bar was eventually completely restored by a Greek family and had become the most expensive hotel on the island, called Bratsera (which translates to "sponge

TWENTIETH
CENTURY-FOX
TELEVISION

3 Feb. 1984
4111 Wade St.
Los Angeles, Calif.
90066

Dear Marianne,

It was so good to hear from you finally. I was beginning to
wonder if my tee-shirts ever reached their intended destinations.
I really felt bad when Maggie told me you were to arrive on Hydra
only a short while after we had left.
It was wonderful to be back there again, after over six years.
Torie loved it too, she spent a lot of time playing with Emily
and she felt very grown-up to be able to walk around the island
by herself whenever she wanted to.
I'm currently working at 20th Century Fox in the TV Syndication
Dept. as a booker. It is okay work and fun being on the lot
and going to the commissary etc. I am also working on a screenplay
which is going quite well. Hope that some of my contacts here will
someday pay off!
Torie is in second grade, 7½ years old, very bright and beautiful - I wish you could meet her. If you were serious about taking
a vacation, please be my guest. I would be delighted to have
you come and stay still living in the big old farmhouse built
by Louis Armstrong about 65 years ago, one of the oldest places
around. We have lots of room - so please think about it.
I am living with a woman, someone I think you would like.
She is kind and supportive, something rather different for me
and we are both planning a return European trip this summer.
(with Torie of course)
We will probably arrive in London toward the middle of Aug.
then on to Rome and Hydra. (Maybe we could meet in London?)
I hear news sometimes from George Lialios, seems like some big
changes on Hydra - also hear from Charlie Gurd, Brandy sometimes
(I thought it was quite ironic when I returned that I spent the
first 3 nights at Jean Marc's place - staying with Charlie until
I could find a place) I often wonder if we will ever all see each other
again. I for one would enjoy it now that I'm old and mellowed.

Life is going well for me - I hope it goes the same for you-
I would like us to keep in touch - the old nostalgia for the
seekers never quite leaves me.
GIve my love to Axel, I know time will take care of things
there - sing and dance and laugh and

Love,
Judy

Fig. 11.

factory"). In 1982, though, it was just a ruined building with only one room still standing. As one entered the site from the exterior door, a quite large room opened to the left. To the right were two washrooms and, in between, a cobblestone path led out to an open field with weeds and wildflowers growing where the sponge factory had once stood.

That year I was witness to (or maybe I should say participant in) one of the most incredible events to occur in Bill's Bar—and that was a pretty high bar (no pun intended). I'd become friendly with another of the island's most famous and popular denizens, Maggie Martin, who was married, at the time, to a very wealthy German shipowner named Gunter. We hung out together a lot that month, and Maggie was crazy about Torie, often buying her expensive presents. Maggie and Gunter always picked up the tab when we were together—something I greatly appreciated.

One day, while we were drinking Polish vodka (with caviar and hard-boiled eggs, of course), we stayed at the bar until the afternoon closing time. After everyone else, including Bill, had retired home for a siesta except for Anthony (who was also a frequent recipient of Maggie and Gunter's generosity), Stefane (pronounced Stefanay), the communist bartender, put on some Greek music, and Maggie and Torie started to dance. Ever exuberant and quite drunk, Gunter got a bunch of plates from the kitchen and threw them one by one on the floor, as the Greeks often did to honor good dancers.

We all thought that was bibulously amusing. When they were all broken, he went and got some more plates and some glasses as well. Long story short: Gunter broke every single plate, glass, and empty bottle in the place. Then I saw him eyeing the liquor bottles behind the bar. At that point, Anthony came over and said to me, "This is going to get nasty—you have to take Torie away."

I was really enjoying the chaos, so I said, "Yeah, okay, I will in a minute."

Fortunately, at that point, Gunter had discovered a few more unbroken glasses in the bar sink, which gave pause to his liquor-bottle intentions. The floor was absolutely covered in broken glasses, dishes, wine bottles, and crockery. Anthony was more insistent now, "If you don't take her out of here, I will!" So, reluctantly, off we went.

When I got back down to Tasso's café and noticed all the fine scratches covering Torie's legs, I realized that Anthony was a much better caretaker at that point than I'd been (though Torie was not really hurt, and the multitude of tiny red marks caused her no pain and were gone by evening). Later, I heard that Anthony helped Gunter and Stefane clean the place up, then the three of them scoured the whole island for replacement glasses and dishes and got them all back to the bar before Bill returned, which—though it mollified Bill to some degree—still left Gunter with a seven-hundred-dollar-plus bar bill.

For many years afterward, people would ask me, "Were you there the day Gunter destroyed Bill's Bar?"

It was kind of a badge of honor. And, after all, no harm, no foul.

That summer, when I rented the little cottage, I again had a near-miss with a big old tarantula. I learned tarantulas hibernate over the winter and resurface in spring. Wouldn't you know it? May is their preferred emergence month.

One day, soon after I took possession of the house, I noticed while sitting on the john that at the base of the wall the tile did not go all the way down to the floor and a long, black leg was peeking out from underneath the tiled overhang. Lucky for me, my Montreal friend, Charlie Gurd, was coming over for dinner. I threw myself on his masculine bravado.

"Charlie, you've got to help me, I think there's a tarantula coming out from under the bathroom tile."

"Show me," he said.

We went into the tiny room where there now were two hairy black legs sticking out. God bless Charlie. He took a large wad of toilet paper, moistened it, and stuck it quickly up under the tile where the two legs instantly disappeared. Then he put more wet paper all along the bottom of the tile and tried to reassure me it was going to be okay.

"Usually," he told me, "they have two exits, one inside and one outside, so probably the spider will just exit into the garden."

I've never peed so quickly as I did for the rest of that month, and thankfully, the tarantula never re-emerged.

I was always on guard for tarantulas and centipedes, always imagining that I'd find one in a shoe or boot (like one sees in jungle movies).

One time, back in 1977, at the Kellogg house after I had dressed Torie and put her in her stroller, I had finished dressing myself. When I picked up my good old Frye boots and started putting one on, my toes felt something soft inside. I jumped up in the air, screaming, and fell back on the bed, furiously kicking at the boot to get it off. I'll never forget Torie's expression as she watched this. It appeared as if she was thinking, *Oh great, my mother has just gone crazy, and I'm stuck here on this Greek island. I can't walk or talk, now what will I do?* I had to laugh just looking at the distress on her little face as I slowly picked up the offending boot and shook it on the floor. Out fell . . . my sock.

Torie just looked at me as if I'd lost my mind.

Around that time—I think it was right after the plate-breaking incident at Bill's Bar—Suzanne returned to Hydra with her French boyfriend and the children, but they weren't there very long. It seems they got caught growing marijuana in the garden or on the patio. I heard that someone she didn't get on with (quel shock) turned her in to the local authorities. I also heard it cost Leonard eighty-thousand dollars to get her out of jail and out of the country (!). She was not permitted to go back for something like ten years, but she did eventually return and stayed in Leonard's house for a long time.

I didn't see Suzanne again until many years later.

When I first brought Monika to Hydra in 1984, I was seriously worried about how Anthony would regard her. She was not an overly creative or intellectual person and, though she had a warm and engaging personality with a very pleasant face and body, she was not anything like a jet-setting fashion model (of which, to be fair, there are many to be found in that part of the world). Monika was still working at her very first job, installing and repairing equipment for the telephone company, and to be honest, I was afraid Anthony might go off on her as well.

Nothing could have been further from the truth, however. In fact, after only a few pleasant evenings together, Anthony declared that he was in love with her! I don't know which of us was more astonished. It did not seem to matter a bit to him that I was witness to these declarations of love. He was totally upfront about it.

"Maybe you could just give me a little kiss good night," he'd say to her.

Poor Monika. She really had no idea how to respond. There never was any kissing, though. Finally, Maggie Martin, who was very close with Anthony (before and after the "Bill's Bar Incident") and often helped him with his expenses, told him to leave Monika alone, and he reluctantly acquiesced.

It taught me something I should have already known. The true value of my lifelong partner lay in her big heart, her pure soul, and her honest-and-true character. I was absolutely humbled to realize that Anthony could see right into that heart and soul and recognize the value.

Maggie owned a house on Hydra that she rented to Anthony and Christina and, after they separated, to Christina and her new lover, Michael. At the point when Maggie intervened to restrain Anthony's pursuit of Monika, she was married to Gunter, who worked for Stavros Niarchos—a rival to Aristotle Onassis for being the richest man in Greece and the most prosperous shipping magnate. Anyway, Gunter got very wealthy from running a shipping service that cleaned supertankers for Niarchos. Both Maggie and Gunter were very generous with all their friends and basically benefactors to Anthony, who, by then, had pretty much run out of money.

Although Alexis had always told me, "If you want to get away with anything on Hydra, don't do it for more than an hour," I was, however, in September of 1984, witness to a small group of conspirators who managed to pull it off.

I nicknamed it "The Great Escape."

One of the earliest ex-pats who made their home on Hydra from the mid-sixties was a British writer named Donald Lowe. He lived at the time of this story in what could only be described as a hovel, even by Hydra standards, with no hot water, heat, or inside toilet (forget about a shower). He was a bit of a reprobate and fairly introverted but could, in fact, be charming when he wanted to (though he seldom did), especially to the fairer sex.

Back in the early eighties, Donald managed to catch the fancy of a young Australian girl named Mandy, who was very attractive with long raven hair and striking blue eyes. She moved in and, subsequently, had two children with him, first a girl named Gemma and, two years later, a boy named Douglas. Being one of those fierce, rugged Outback-type Aussies, Mandy gave birth with just a Greek midwife in attendance.

Mandy was much more social than Donald, and everyone really liked her, but things did not go well. Don began to drink heavily, and after a time, Mandy wanted to leave Hydra and return home to Australia, but he wouldn't hear of it. No one was taking his children away, he proclaimed. When Mandy got word from her sister that their mother had cancer and was probably dying, things really came to a head. Donald became physically abusive and, when Mandy appeared at Mother's Beach one day with a black eye, the whole foreign colony became deeply concerned for her welfare.

So two of the most preeminent ex-pat members, Helen Marden and Jean Marc, hatched a plan: They went into Athens and somehow got Gemma's and Dougie's pictures attached to Mandy's Australian passport and then booked tickets for her and the kids to return to Sydney. I was staying on the island at the time but knew nothing about this—one of the few times something was carried out on Hydra and no one else was in on it.

I do remember seeing Mandy walk through the port on that fateful day, very quickly, with a basket on her arm and the kids in tow, heading for the quay. Someone sitting with us at Tasso's commented that she was going on a picnic with Helen, Colby, and her son, Alexander. We didn't think anything of it because the quay, besides being where the hydrofoils docked, was also where you got picnic boats to take you up the coast to Bisti, where there were both a very nice sandy beach and a picnic area. It's just that Mandy looked so serious, almost to the point of being frightened.

Eventually, I lost track of the would-be picnickers, did some shopping, and, several hours later, settled back at our customary table at Tasso's only to behold Donald positively flying through the port, headed for the hydrofoil office. He managed to catch the last boat into Piraeus, and as he departed, the true story of what was going on emerged. Mandy had left everything—all their clothes and belongings—at the shack where they lived. But one thing she had to take with her was her passport.

When Donald discovered it missing, he knew instantly that he'd been played. It was almost like watching a suspense thriller.

We had to wait until the next morning to find out that Mandy had made it to Hellinikon Airport in time for her plane—Donald got there just in time to see it take off. What a relief we all felt! We were pretty sure he would've killed her had he arrived in time . . . but he didn't.

It seemed like a classic case of someone inadvertently manifesting their worst fear. If he had just let her go to visit her dying mother, she probably would've come back to him.

The Stagecoach was another one of those Athens hangouts popular with the ex-pat crowd. Located on a side street in Kolonaki, it was owned by a Greek man named Nick and his British wife, Annie. It was famous for serving prime rib dinners with all the English fixings, including Yorkshire pudding. Monika and I would go there every time we visited Greece either on our way to Hydra or returning home. Since we'd become very friendly with Nick and Annie over the years, we'd stay long after closing, sitting at the bar with them and their obnoxious (and noxious) boxer dog, Prince, drinking up the night for free as their guests.

One night in particular is etched in memory: We'd spent two months in Europe, one traveling around and one in our house, Poet's Corner on Hydra. Back in those days (circa 1987), airfares from Greece were quite expensive, as Olympic Airlines had a monopoly on all routes in and out of the country. But I, being the clever world traveler, knew you could purchase very cheap round-trip charter fares in London from what were known as "bucket shops." I had a friend in London buy us three tickets, intending to only use the returns. It would've saved us six hundred dollars over the one-way fare on Olympic. The friend posted the tickets to us, and we picked them up from the American Express office in Athens. I was so proud of myself for circumventing the onerous Greek travel restrictions. Alas—it was they who outsmarted me.

The charter flights all left in the middle of the night, so we stayed at the Stagecoach until about one a.m. and then taxied to Hellinikon Airport (how I miss it). We got in the queue for our flight at three a.m. and presented our passports and tickets to the desk agent, where they were quickly snatched up by a woman representing Olympic Airlines. She noted that our entry stamp in our passports was not from Athens but via Corfu. She quickly motioned the baggage handler to pull our bags off the conveyer belt.

"What are you doing?!" I shouted at her.

"You did not arrive from this ticket, so you cannot use it to depart," she declared.

Many glasses of red wine had not enhanced my wits, so I replied, "It was a mix-up. There was a strike in Italy, and we couldn't get to London for the flight, so we came directly to Greece via the ferry from Brindisi." (This part at least was true.)

"You will have to go speak with the head of the airport," she told me and directed me to a small basement office deep in the bowels of Hellinikon.

The good news? The head of the airport spoke English.

The bad news? He didn't buy my story for a minute.

"You bought these tickets here in Nikis Street [where all the travel agencies in Athens were located], didn't you?" he asked, accusingly.

"No! They were sent to us by a friend. We picked them up today from the American Express," I insisted.

Fortunately, I had the envelope with the British stamp and post-mark in my purse.

"Please," I implored. "My daughter is only eleven and is sleeping upstairs on the marble floor. Please let us get on our flight."

He seemed to hesitate, and I thought he might relent—but then he asked me a fateful (as it turned out) question: "Where did you stay in Athens?"

Without thinking (the damn wine again), I answered truthfully: "We stayed at the Grande Bretagne."

(The most expensive hotel in Athens at the time—which my connections to a travel agent on Hydra got us a room for half the going rate.)

That did it for him. "No!" he yelled. "You can afford to pay for a scheduled flight!"

I pleaded, begged, even cried—but he would not relent. Heartsick, I returned to the departure terminal where Monika and Torie were waiting for me with the now discharged luggage (all seven bags). The earliest scheduled flight to London was an Air Kenya flight at six-thirty in the morning. I booked three tickets using my American Express card. It cost me $1,500.00, almost the cost of our round-trip United tickets from Los Angeles to London.

Live and learn—but ouch!

That was a painfully expensive lesson, so it didn't bother me at all when Olympic went bankrupt several years later due to mismanagement and corrupt business practices.

In 1990, Monika and I spent the month of August on Hydra with Torie (who was then fourteen) and our close Greek American friend, Dena Bouskos. Brian and Valerie's house was already spoken for, so we rented the "crash pad" owned by the Brownings. They'd fixed it up and made it very comfortably habitable since the old hippie days in the seventies when it really was a crash pad.

One evening, we were all eating dinner at Pyrofani's (or what preceded Pyrofani's—it was definitely a taverna, but Theo, our dear friend who has owned it for many years, was not yet the proprietor), and we saw a bunch of very young children tormenting a tiny kitten. They were tossing it at a little girl who was shrieking in mock horror.

After several not-so-gentle tosses, I got up and grabbed the kitten from them and told them in Greek, "Min!" which means "Don't!"

I brought the kitten, which was not at all injured by the somewhat rough treatment, over to our table. Although it was very young, perhaps only four or five weeks old, it ate the *keftedes* (meatballs) and drank the *gala* (milk) we gave him without hesitation. We asked the waiter if he knew where the mother cat was.

He shrugged and said, "They drop them off here all the time."

So Frank (because he had blue eyes) joined our household.

When we brought him up to the house, we put a towel in a straw basket and put it out on our patio. Frank cuddled into it as soon as we placed him in it, and lo and behold, the next morning, he was still there. Frank, like all the other Hydra cats, young as he was, knew a good thing when he found it.

So began our crusade to persuade Dena that she absolutely needed her own Greek cat. It took some convincing and some assistance from the other ex-pats. But a health certificate was obtained, and Frank was flown by yet another friend, Susie Jacobs, who lived on Hydra but was from Los Angeles, to our house in LA where Dena, after completing a business trip to New York, picked him up—but not before he'd spent his last night in Greece at the Grande Bretagne Hotel in Athens with internationally famous artist Brice Marden and his wife, Helen, and their two daughters. Frank lived happily ever after, with Dena doting on him, until his eighteenth year.

In 1996, after a gap of several years, I saw Alexis Bolens in the bar of Bratsera, the nicest hotel on Hydra, with his then wife, Colby, whom I hadn't seen in over twenty years.

I didn't notice them at first when I entered the bar with Monika and a friend who came with us after we had all attended the Cannes Film Festival. I was sitting with my back to the room, so when Alexis came up to us and whispered in my ear, "Are we both so old now we don't recognize one another?" I turned and smiled with delight, so glad he remembered Black Bart's girl once again.

I joined them for a drink at their table, and he regaled me with stories of their son, Alexander, who was seventeen at the time and growing up, "even taller than me," Alexis said with pride. They'd sold the big house with the swimming pool built into the cliff. He and Colby now lived with Alexander in Geneva where Colby worked to support them. I'm not sure that Alexis had ever worked since managing that coffee plantation. I remember him saying to me once before, "I came so close, so close to being fabulously rich. But it never happened."

Two years later, I heard some terrible news. After Colby and Alexis had split up, their son Alexander committed suicide at the age of nineteen for no apparent reason. He got his father's gun from the cabinet in their apartment, went into the bathroom, and shot himself in the head. That's where his mother found him when she returned from work. And that awful tragedy was compounded six months later when Colby did the exact same thing, with the same gun. Alexis wasn't there at the time. He was in Athens living with Lena, the Greek ex-wife of Bill Cunliffe, another renowned habitué and owner of Bill's Bar, from Hydra.

In 2006, Monika and I arranged to rent George Lialios' house to celebrate my sixtieth birthday. Three old friends from England and one from Japan shared the cost of the rental with us. Lindsey Callicoatt was there as well, staying at Brice and Helen Marden's.

Lindsey and I have been friends now for over thirty-eight years. Monika has become a very good friend of his as well, and so has my daughter, Torie. He was/is one of the most beloved ex-pats on Hydra.

He is very attractive in a kind of artistic/poetic way, with dirty blonde hair and blue eyes. And his demeanor is soft and engaging without being at all effeminate. He was born in 1948 in Oxnard, California, and raised in Culver City, where I now live. He has worked in many different professions (kind of like me). He's been a teacher, a carpenter, and, for many years, worked as a stained-and-etched-glass artisan in a business that an ex-lover started in San Francisco. His popularity has much to do with the fact that he is endlessly interested in everyone and everything he encounters and has a way of making each person feel appreciated and valued.

Although Lindsey considered himself primarily gay, he just couldn't resist an occasional tryst with an attractive lady. And one of them was Betsy Van Dyke, who spent several years in the late seventies on Hydra as manager of the Saudi's house (the old Cavos disco) and where she and Lindsey had a long and dramatic affair. She was quite attractive, witty, and very bright, just Lindsey's type. In no time at all, Betsy was pregnant. Their son, Peter, was born in 1980 on Hydra at Helen's house where they were living. And after they'd returned to the States, they had a second son, two years later, named Nico.

Lindsey recalled for me the arc of his time on Hydra:

It was October 1970. I was twenty-three and going to a new place to do a job I was untrained to do. Was I scared and lonely? Probably, I don't remember. But I was going to the island of Leonard Cohen! There was a comfort in that. I will spare you my story of discovering his music and poetry, but will say that when I got a one-way ticket to Europe the previous June, my one bag contained record albums by him.

I met Anne and Harold Ramis (the famous movie screenwriter/ director/actor of *Ghostbusters* fame) on a cloudy November day in some obscure lane. He was tall, curly haired, and hot. She was hard to peg with her amusing original thought patterns. She has a fascinating way of speaking—to this day I can't properly describe it but still love it. She'd be famous for it if she were an actress. She also wore a big hat so she wouldn't have to say hello to people unless she wanted to. He wasn't a famous filmmaker yet. He'd been a joke editor for *Playboy*, and I imagine had done his Second City days, but I didn't know what that was then. Later, they brought me to a rehearsal of *SNL*, where I met Gilda Radner. Jane Curtin called me Mister Sincere, which I don't think was a compliment. Anne and Harold were the first of many important friendships that began on Hydra. Many of these people were life-altering (in the best of ways). Almost everyone I care about I met there, or through people I met there. It was a place that attracted minds, hearts, talents, beauty (physical and in the soul). I fell in love regularly. Besides attracting these people, Hydra put you together with them. No cars! You met them in the lane, at the post office, on the swimming rocks, in tavernas, on the boat from Athens. One only had to go out the door, and there they'd be. One afternoon, passing through the port, I sat down with Anne and Harold at Tasso's. "Come to celebrity watch?" Harold asked, moving his eyes to the left. Draped in a nearby chair was Jackie O, white pants suit, signature sunglasses. She'd helicoptered in to look at one of Hydra's mansions, possibly to buy it. She gracefully tapped the arm of the chair next her and said, "furniture." Why after more than fifty years would I remember a banal utterance by a moderately attractive (though stylish) woman? Because she had been the Queen of our empire. Her Chanel suit had been covered in her husband's blood. The dear woman had carried on best she could, and now she was considering how to make a house comfy. I think that's why. The first spring, my household was comprised of four lovely women and me. I shared my bed with Hedva, who was Israeli. She had a ring on every finger and gave me the best one. I have many friends who are men and loved some. I especially like the artists, the painters. They are like trees. But women interest me so much more. They keep me fascinated, the smart ones most of all. I never understand them completely (part of what I like), but I think I understand them more than most men do, or can, or try to. I like women the way I like color: infinite, making life worthwhile. Also, they tend to be much more fun. I doubt I'd be so obsessed with movies if it weren't for the actresses.

I see Hydra as feminine: the endless lanes of discovery, the way the harbor envelops one on arrival. The island beckons women. It's civilized. They are not harassed. They bloom in that backdrop. And I was able to reap many of them. Some lovers, all friends, they nourish my spirit to this day.

There are rocks that rise from the sea, at that point. Rounding a promontory of the Peloponnese, one gets the first view of Hydra, far off, shrouded by mists. Those rocks resemble reptilian monsters. To me they seem to be guarding a dream. Every time I return, I wonder if it was. Seriously, I do.

—Lindsey Callicoatt, 2015

One day, Monika and I were walking to the port and ran into Brian Sidaway standing talking to Suzanne Elrod at the foot of Donkey Shit Lane. She is two years younger than I am, so she must've been about fifty-eight at the time, but she was walking with a cane.

Brian greeted us, and we stopped to chat for a moment. Pointing to Suzanne, he asked me, "Do you two know each other?" Having no interest in acknowledging her, I shook my head no, and so did she.

"Judy this is Suzanne; Suzanne this is Judy."

We both pretended we did not recognize one another, but there is no doubt in my mind she well knew who I was. I muttered, "Hello," and turned back immediately to Brian.

"We are going down to Tasso's to meet Lindsey," I said.

"Oh," Suzanne exclaimed, "Lindsey! I'd love to see Lindsey again!"

I ignored her and just said so long to Brian.

Several days later, on our way to the bar in the Bratsera Hotel, Lindsey and I passed her sitting at a little elevated café. I heard her call out to him, but Lindsey is deaf in one ear and did not hear her. I told him, "Suzanne is calling you," and pointed to where she was sitting. I added, "I'll meet you at the bar," and kept on walking.

After that, I saw her several times on Hydra, from a distance, looking old and miserable.

In 2008, I ran into Jean Noel (the gay artist I originally met in 1975 who Suzanne had the unrequited crush on back then) in the port. He was there to attend his good friend Lily Mac's funeral, which I also attended. Lily was quite old when she passed and was a real fixture on Hydra. She was of Russian extraction, born in Iran, and had arrived in Greece in the late forties. She was reputed to be the first foreign woman to live on Hydra by herself. In her earlier years, while still living in Athens, she also had the reputation of being the most beautiful woman in Greece. George Lialios and another Hydra regular, Pandias Skaramanga (the ex-president of the Bank of Greece), were both known to have pursued her passionately at the time. Anyway, that was years before she settled in Kamini on Hydra and made friends with so many of the island's residents.

After the funeral, Jean Noel, a Parisian friend of his, and I sat at Tasso's and tried to catch up on over thirty years. He'd become an artist and showed me pictures of some papier-machè puppets he'd made, very creative and original. He mentioned Suzanne, who was still on Hydra, only a few hundred yards away, in fact, at Leonard's house.

I tried to encourage him to drop in on her. By then, she had alienated most of the foreigners on the island (including me), and I thought she might enjoy an old flame's visit. But he again demurred.

"No," he said, "I don't think so. She came to visit once, some years ago, to my loft in Paris. It was very . . . awkward."

Finally, in 2009 or 2010, she decided to leave the island for good and return to Florida where, she declared, "People still care about me."

It was during that period that another horrible woman in Leonard Cohen's life (his personal manager) stole all his life savings, forcing him to go back on the road at the age of seventy-seven. He'd always been extremely popular in Europe and played to many sold-out venues. One of those shows was held in Athens. While he was in Greece, I heard that he'd sent word that Suzanne would not be welcome at his concert. Their daughter, Lorca, who was accompanying the tour as the stills-photographer, actually took some of the crew out to Hydra before they left the country but didn't attempt to see her mother who was living just two-hundred yards up the hill.

After hearing that, I wrote to Marianne:

"Dostoevsky maintains that hell is the inability to love. When I think of that, the first person who comes to mind is Suzanne."

Marianne wrote back, referring to that quotation and adding: "You are a true friend."

How existentially horrible it must be to know that when you die, no one will mourn you. Whatever cruelties, or spiteful acts, or just plain bad mistakes one has made, I don't think anyone deserves that fate. Not even Suzanne.

Marianne and I were finally reunited on Hydra after almost thirty-five years. Over many trips, I had hoped to find her again, and many of them, we just missed one another by a week or two.

But in 2011, we'd contacted one another via Facebook. There are things to be grateful for on Facebook, and finding long-lost friends and lovers was at the top of my list. We corresponded and arranged to take our vacations at the same time. So, sitting with Monika at Tasso's at our old familiar table, I saw Marianne walking through the port with her then husband, Jan. I got up and ran to her calling her name, and just like that, we were once again embracing after so many years, together again!

They came and joined us for a drink. While Jan was inside, Marianne leaned over and said to Monika, "I'm going to steal her from you! But just for one day."

We all laughed at that; Marianne was ever the flirt—although Monika was not terribly amused.

We arranged to meet up the next day, just the two of us, at Pyrofani's in Kamini and go for lunch. We walked the inside road to Vlicho and sat at the little taverna there. Marianne's authorized biography had just been translated and published in English, and in typical fashion, Marianne expressed serious reservations about having her life story exposed so publicly. To be honest, I'd already read a copy, and knowing what I knew about her life, I found it extremely sanitized and not very engaging. Especially in comparison to all the really interesting and detailed stories she had confided to me.

But I couldn't help asking her about one curious, inaccurate detail in the book: her encounter with Suzanne and subsequent departure from Hydra and the house she would never again occupy.

"Marianne," I began, "why did you say in the book that Suzanne arrived with Adam as an infant, the same age as Axel was when you moved in with Leonard? Adam was four when Suzanne moved here and caused you to leave your house. It was Lorca who was the infant at the time. She was eleven months old."

Marianne looked very confused and asked, "Well, which one of them is older?"

"Adam is three years older than Lorca," I said. "And why did you say you took Axel and left immediately? Axel was still here when I arrived two weeks after your departure. Remember? I had to buy him a ticket when he lost the one you gave him and you paid me back when I came to Oslo to visit you later that year."

She just shook her head. "You know," she said, "there were phone calls and Leonard offered to buy me another house, but . . ." Her voice trailed off. "It was all so painful. I guess I blocked it out for a while."

She did look really distressed and took another sip of her wine. I almost regretted bringing it up then; it was that old *Jeopardy* contestant in me: Judy, with the phenomenal memory, still a stickler for accurately recalled details.

"Ah, well," I said, "it doesn't really matter anymore, does it? I guess no one really got what they wanted out of the whole mess."

She smiled then and emphatically agreed.

We spent the rest of the afternoon drinking wine and reminiscing. I asked about Axel, though I knew from others that he was not well. He had been committed for life to a mental facility in Oslo after having suffered a nervous breakdown at the age of seventeen. She sighed again.

"He is suffering, and it's all my fault. I can do nothing to help him. Sometimes when I visit, he seems fine, just like the Axel before . . . but sometimes, he is so angry and bitter and has to be restrained from destroying everything in his room."

I didn't know what to offer or what to say, except: "Marianne, it wasn't your fault. You did the best you could." His father was mentally ill too, and that kind of illness is often inherited. But I knew how she felt, at least a little bit. I, too, felt guilty over Axel, for not being more of a responsible adult, not keeping him from taking mind-altering drugs, not protecting him more—or at least paying more attention. Yeah, I felt guilty too. I still do. There were so many young ones who were collateral damage.

We talked of other things that were less troubling. We had years and years of catching up to do. Then we walked back up the coast road to Kamini, where she and Jan were staying at Kyria Sophia's guesthouse.

"Come up and see our room," she said. We climbed the outdoor stairs to a very modest room where Jan was reading a Norwegian newspaper on the small balcony.

"Isn't it a lovely view?" Marianne asked me.

It *was* a lovely view—but I couldn't quite get over how much had changed in her life. She was now almost seventy-seven. I was saddened by how much Marianne herself had changed and how much she had been short-changed.

The very last time I saw Marianne was on Hydra in May of 2013. She was once again with Jan (there had been problems), and they were there with his daughters and their families to celebrate one daughter's fiftieth birthday. Monika and I were with my filmmaking godson, Christian, and his fiancé, Athena, who joined us after attending the Cannes Film Festival. Chris, Athena, Monika, and I shared a house that I'd found online, the Gore/Booth House that had once been owned by the British ambassador to India. It was located high up on the right side of the port close to where our old friend, Pandias (who was in his nineties) had his house.

Once again, we met up with Marianne in the port at Tasso's and made a date to come up to our place for lunch the next day. We lunched on our rooftop terrace. Pandias spotted us from his terrace, and he invited us to come up and see all of Anthony Kingsmill's paintings, which he had hanging throughout his house. He had won them from Anthony long before playing those infamous poker games. We did go up then, and Pandias very kindly allowed me to take photos of many of Anthony's paintings. I had to promise they'd be for my own personal use, and later, I had some of them enlarged and framed. They've joined all the other Hydra artists we collected over the years. All the others are originals that we purchased, of course.

We also dined out at Marianne's favorite taverna, Christina's in Kamini. But that time, unfortunately, we were both very involved with our own little *parea* (social group), so no long walks to Vlicho or long, bittersweet reminiscences or intimate conversations. Still, it was wonderful to see her again, and she looked so healthy and content in her life at last.

When we left Hydra, after two weeks, Marianne invited us to come and visit her in Norway, and we promised that on our next European visit, we'd include a visit to Oslo. We were standing at the quay, awaiting the hydrofoil that would take us back to Athens. When it arrived, Marianne hugged me and kissed my cheeks and, as Monika and Jan helped to load the luggage onboard, I hugged her one last time and whispered in her ear: "I have always loved you."

She smiled that old familiar smile and waved goodbye.

EPILOGUE

I tried keeping in touch with Leonard, but as more and more time elapsed, and after I moved West, our communication grew more infrequent.

Still, any time I did contact him, he always responded right away. In 1987, Monika, Torie, and I did an extended European vacation (two months), culminating in a month at B&V's Poet's Corner house on Hydra. We'd purchased one of the first consumer videotape cameras, and we did some pretty extensive filming with Anthony and some of our other Hydra friends. When Anthony passed away two years later, Lindsey and I developed an idea for a documentary about him. I had about eight hours of candid video, and once we had a pretty good "pitch" package, I wrote to Leonard (who at this point was again with the Roshi on Mount Baldy) and asked for his assistance.

As always, he called me right away.

"Anthony was a very great man," he said. "Use my name whatever way it works for you. And we can discuss using some of my music—if it gets to that point."

I was so flustered by his unhesitating generosity that I stammered out a few words of gratitude and promised to keep him posted on our progress. While in London the following year, I pitched the project to the BBC, and they took it "under consideration." After six months, though, I received my pitch package back from the BBC exec who was evaluating it. "It was a close call," the rejection letter stated, "but in the end, all the notable Brits in the project are deceased and having an American producer attached did not work for us either." And that was the end of that. I still have the video footage, and some years ago, I had the VHS converted to DVD format. Maybe someday I'll get to include it somewhere—who knows?

December of 2009 was the last time I saw Leonard. It was at his house on Tremaine Avenue in a fairly nondescript neighborhood just south of Pico Boulevard and east of Highland Avenue in Los Angeles. A mutual friend of ours, Hazel, had left her video camera on Hydra several months before, and through a series of convoluted transfers, it had come into my possession in LA. Hazel phoned me once she found out I'd located it and asked if I could drop it off at Leonard's house as a guest of his was returning the next day to Montreal and she'd deliver it to Hazel.

I was advised to just leave it on the upstairs landing if Leonard didn't answer the door and was prepared to do just that. I'd kept in very loose touch with him over the years (e.g., the proposed Anthony Kingsmill documentary that Leonard was so supportive of but that never got made).

I'd brought along my friend, Cedering Fox (a professional voiceover artist who had been the announcer for the Academy Awards Show and also the Democratic Convention and is the founder and director of Word Theater, one of the most acclaimed spoken word series in the world).

We were on our way to a Christmas Party nearby, given by our indie film friends Bobby and Kerry Rock. When I knocked on the door, Leonard answered right away. He came out onto the small porch and gave me a loving embrace.

"It's been a long time, hasn't it?" I asked.

He invited me into the apartment and offered me some *retsina* wine. I told him I had a friend waiting for me down in the car. "Bring her up," he invited, and I rushed back down the stairs. "Leonard wants to meet you." She parked the car and followed me up the stairs.

I took his latest book (*The Book of Longing*) with me and asked him to sign it, which he very graciously did. We stayed about a half hour, and Leonard was his usual gracious self, sharing hummus, crackers, and wine with us. We reminisced, and I reminded him of that drunken night with Anthony and "Danny Boy" and "Kevin Barry."

He smiled. "I think I remember that," he said.

"It was a magic time, wasn't it?"

He nodded. "Yes," he said, softly, "it was."

As we were leaving, I turned to him and said, "I always hoped I'd meet you again."

Putting his arms around me and pulling me close, he said, "Now you have."

I hugged him back.

"Now I have."

One of my favorite LC songs is "Famous Blue Raincoat":

And you treated my woman to a flake of your life.
And when she came back she was nobody's wife*

That's how my time with Leonard and Marianne felt; once upon a time, I shared a brief, but so precious, flake of their very full, very eventful lives. And even though I was not totally changed or transformed, it did give me something I'd never really had: a new feeling of self-worth and self-confidence.

---

* "Famous Blue Raincoat," Leonard Cohen

I found my sexuality—not a small thing—at a time when, despite the cultural upheaval of the day, conformity was very much the norm and coming out took real courage. If we're put with people to learn certain lessons, it can be said that Leonard and Marianne taught me well.

There's something almost magical about knowing and being accepted for who you are by a genius, especially a poetic, musical genius. It's not exactly a spiritual experience but something just as impactful. It's transformative and truly life-changing. It never leaves you and, if you're as lucky as I was, it stays with you in a very profound way. It leaves you feeling like, *I may not be all that much myself, but I was once a good friend and confidante of an exceptional, once-in-a-century man. And he cared for me and remembered me over all the years.*

And I knew him to be kind and caring and generous and oh-so-funny and playful and yet sad and sincere and serious all at the same time. That he was able to galvanize all those myriad, contradictory states of mind and emotion over so many years into beautiful works of music and poetry is a testament to his enduring genius.

Apart from that one six-year hiatus from 1976 to 1982, I've returned to Hydra every two years or so since that first fateful trip in 1973. It remains a magical place, filled with beauty and music and laughter and all kinds of stimulation. And the people! There is always someone new to meet and some old friend—not seen for years and years—to reconnect with.

I wound up knowing Alexis Bolens for over forty years. I'm pretty sure I've actually seen him every time I've been to Hydra. The last time was on my twentieth or maybe twenty-fifth trip there. Monika and I were sitting having dinner with our friends Lindsey and Nico in Kamini at Pyrofani's, a kind of hybrid—part taverna, part bistro—run by a very friendly Greek named Theo who works on Hydra half the year these days and lives in London with his wife and children the other half.

Alexis came down the stairs into the little *platia* (square) with a Greek lady friend and sat at a nearby table. After a bit, he got up and came over to us and reached over to take my hand.

"I didn't see you there!" he said. "The light was shining in my eyes."

I told him, "I'm so happy we ran into you!"

Of course, I understood perfectly—that light shining in all of our eyes. The Hydra light that shines despite the tragedies endured.

The memories linger of the ones no longer with us: Anthony Kingsmill, his ex-wife Christina who died of cancer tragically early at forty-two, Bill Cunliffe of Bill's Bar, George Lialios, Maggie Martin, Jane Motley, Dimitri Gassoumis, Skip Milson, Tasso Katsika—the café proprietor and confidante to all . . . the list is quite long and grows with each passing year.

And now, so tragically premature, Leonard Cohen and Marianne Ihlen . . . gone, but never, ever forgotten. Another famous singer/song-writer, Paul Simon, gave us this very good piece of advice:

Long ago it must be, I have a photograph
Preserve your memories, They're all that's left you.*

These are my memories.

---

* "Old Friends/Bookends," Paul Simon

ACKNOWLEDGMENTS

My sincere thanks and gratitude for their friendship, support, and assistance go to John Zervos, Brian Sidaway, Valerie Lloyd Sidaway, Tom Carlisle, Charlotte Gusay, and Robert Morgan Fisher.

Special thanks go to Tordis Hveem, the Executrix of the Marianne Ihlen Estate, for granting me permission to publish her letters and for returning to me my letters to her, and to Axel Joachim Jensen, who also assented his permission. Also to Lindsey Callicoatt for allowing reprint of his diary excerpts and use of his photos, and to Felicity Fanjoy for allowing reprint of her poem "Leaving with Judith."

To my dear life-partner, spouse, and enduring love: Monika Rogasch.

And to the light of my life and angel of my morning—Victoria (Torie) Mary (Scott) Duro and her adorable children Zane River Duro and Sedona Elizabeth Duro.

Finally, I'd like to thank the incredible editing team at Backbeat Books—John Cerullo, Carol Flannery, and Barbara Claire—for their invaluable assistance in getting this project to print.

APPENDIX

MUSIC

Music was always so important to me, providing a soundtrack for my life. These are the albums I listened to, over and over, on George Lialios' stereo in 1973 and then the little single-speaker record player in Lindsey's house in 1975, during my initial visits to Hydra:

Title	Artist
David Whiffen	David Whiffen
Elton John	Elton John (his first album)
Spirit in the Dark	Aretha Franklin
Songs from a Room	Leonard Cohen
Songs of Love and Hate	Leonard Cohen
The Silver Tongued Devil and I	Kris Kristofferson
Whales & Nightingales	Judy Collins
McCartney	Paul McCartney
Every Picture Tells a Story	Rod Stewart
The Temptations in a Mellow Mood	The Temptations
Court and Spark	Joni Mitchell
Hair	American cast album

Title	**Artist**
Sticky Fingers	The Rolling Stones
Candles in the Rain	Melanie
Parsley, Sage, Rosemary and Thyme	Simon & Garfunkel
Evergreen, Vol. 2	Stone Poneys
Also Spake Zarathustra	Richard Strauss
A Man and A Woman	movie soundtrack
Barbarella	movie soundtrack
Sweet Baby James	James Taylor
Scheherazade	Rimsky-Korsakov
New York Tendaberry	Laura Nyro
Goodbye and Hello	Tim Buckley
Starsailor	Tim Buckley
Where Did Everyone Go?	Nat King Cole
Fire Music	Archie Shepp
Wiedersehen mit Marlene	Marlene Dietrich
David's Album	Joan Baez

BOOKS

And these are the books I read during that time:

Title	**Author**
The Greek Passion	Nikos Kazantzakis
The Charioteer	Mary Renault
Zen and the Art of Motorcycle Maintenance	Robert Pirsig

Title	Author
Desolation Angels	Jack Kerouac
Two Sisters	Gore Vidal
The City and the Pillar	Gore Vidal
Briefing for a Descent Into Hell	Doris Lessing
Lady Chatterley's Lover	D. H. Lawrence
The Alexandria Quartet	Lawrence Durrell
One Hundred Years of Solitude	Gabriel García Márquez
Ravages	Violette Leduc
Report to Greco	Nikos Kazantzakis
Between the Acts	Virginia Woolf

WHO'S WHO

The following list may be helpful as a guide to the many people who are mentioned in this memoir. The entries are in alphabetical order by first name because not all surnames are stated in the book.

Adam Cohen—Leonard Cohen's son
Adam Shapiro—a Jewish artist from Montreal who lives on Hydra
Alexander—son of Colby (Kobi) and Alexis Bolens
Alexis Bolens—husband of Colby (Kobi), father of Alexander
Alison Gold—author, longtime Hydra homeowner
Angelika—George Lialios' German wife
Angeliki—George Lialios' Greek housekeeper
Anita—Swiss German astrologer living in Greece
Anne Ramis—glamorous wife of Harold Ramis

Anne Rivers—a writer from Texas residing on Hydra for many years

Anthony Kingsmill—British artist, husband of Christina, father of Emily

Athena—elder daughter of Dimitri Gassoumis

Audrey Browning—wife of Robert, interested in the occult

Axel Joachim Jensen—Marianne's son by Norwegian author Axel Jensen

Baba Ji—Indian spiritual leader

Barbara Neogi—former model, Hydra homeowner, mother of Jeff Brown

Betsy—sometime partner of Lindsey Callicoatt and mother of his two sons, Peter and Nico

Bill Cunliffe—owner of Bill's Bar, ex-husband of Lena, father of Kathy and Caroline

Bill Finley—a notorious gay man formerly married to a Vanderbilt and a Cunard

Brandy Ayre—musician from Montreal, friend of Leonard's

Brian Sidaway—husband of Valerie, Australian, long-term resident of Hydra

Brice Marden—world-renowned minimalist artist, husband of Helen

Boubulina—historic Greek heroine who fought against the Turks

Carol—American travelling companion of Jim Donnelly, ex of Marvin

Cassandra—younger daughter of Dimitri Gassoumis

Cathy—American caretaker of ex-pats' homes on Hydra

Charlie Gurd—architect and artist, a friend of Leonard's from Montreal

Christina—American wife of Anthony Kingsmill, mother of Emily (with Anthony) and Derek (with Michael), lover of Michael

Chuck Hulse—Gordon Merrick's long-term partner, brother of Larry Hulse

Cindy—the author's sister

Constantine Zinnis—nephew of George Lialios

Craig—an American doing an international residency in pediatrics, husband of Sharon

Deidre Dowman—Australian girlfriend of Dimitri Gassoumis

Dena Bouskos—a Greek American friend living in LA

Diana—George Slater's girlfriend

Dimitra—a real-estate agent on Hydra

Dimitri—Greek husband of astrologer Anita

Dimitri Gassoumis—a Greek American artist, father of Athena and Cassandra

Doctor Armand—Jean's Parisian neighbour who was planning a trip to Greece

Donald Lowe—British writer living on Hydra

Emily Kingsmill—daughter of Anthony and Christina

Eva Kellogg—cornflake heiress and owner of a house on Hydra

Felicity Fanjoy—a friend from Montreal

French Minister of Culture—a good friend of Jean Marc Appert

George Lialios—Judy's first friend on Hydra, husband of Angelika, generous homeowner

George Slater—poet, yacht captain, lothario, partner of Diana

Gil Simmons—heir to Simmons mattress fortune, rumored to be working for the CIA

Gordon Merrick—Chuck Hulse's partner, American homoerotic novelist

Gunter—husband of Maggie Martin, got rich working for Stavros Niarchos

Guy—a college friend of James

Gwen—another American caretaker of foreigners' homes on Hydra

Harold Ramis—famous film actor/director/writer, comedian, husband of Anne

Helen Marden—wife of Brice, Hydra homeowner

Helga—Austrian friend of George Lialios, mother of Michel

James—Torie's father, college roommate of Nisette's brother

Jane Motley—American artist, girlfriend of Richard (Rick) Vick

Jean—brother of Judy's college friend Mary-Luc, living with his wife in Paris

Jean Marc Appert—longtime lover of Marianne

Jean Noel—Suzanne's gay crush

Jeff Brown—Barbara Neogi's son, filmmaker, a good friend of Vivi and Vibe

Jim—Leslie's partner

Jim Donnelly—brother of Rosemary, travelling companion of Carol

John Taurek—another of Rita's lovers and friend of Terence, also a philosophy professor

John Zervos—friend of George Lialios, founder of the Athens Centre, partner of Rosemary Donnelly

Judith "Judy" Scott—the author of this memoir

Kari and Mari—Norwegian twin sisters

Kathy—an old friend of Judy who visited from America

Kathy Cunliffe—daughter of Bill and Lena

Kim Clarke—singer/songwriter who used the stage name Bartholomew Neddings

Kobi (Colby)—wife of Alexis Bolens, mother of Alexander

Larry Hulse—younger brother of Chuck Hulse

Lefteris—a Greek bank clerk who married a Swiss woman

Lena—Greek ex-wife of Bill Cunliffe, mother of Kathy and Caroline, later lover of Alexis Bolens

Leonard Cohen—world famous singer/songwriter/writer/poet from Montreal

Lily Mac—a woman from Russia who made her home and died on Hydra

Lindsey Callicoatt—co-author and friend of Judy Scott

Lorca Cohen—Leonard's daughter

Madame Pauori—grande dame of Hydra, pictured (as Bouboulina) on the 1000-drachma banknote

Maggie Martin—homeowner on Hydra, wife of Gunter

Mandy—Australian lover of Donald Lowe, mother of Gemma and Dougie

Marianne Ihlen—Leonard's early partner and muse, mother of Axel

Marilyn—George Lialios' American housekeeper

Marsha Picaud—a former lover of Richard Brautigan, living in Athens

Marvin—Chicago lawyer, ex of Carol whom he tried to kill

Mette Jakobssen—beautiful young woman from Norway, lover of Jean Marc

Michael—lover of Christina Kingsmill after she broke up with Anthony

Michel—Helga's son

Mick—Kathy's gay friend

Monika—Judy's long-term partner

Naná—a Greek American woman who owned a house on Hydra

Nick and Annie—owners of The Stagecoach Restaurant in Athens

Nico—a friend of Lindsey

Nisette Brennan—an American sculptor living in Athens

Palmer—a homeowner on Hydra

Pandias Skaramanga—a retired president of the Bank of Greece

Paul Desmond—Irish poet friend of Anthony and Marianne

Philemon—a friendly donkey man, son of the ranting woman

Philip—young gay Australian, who had a crush on Lindsey

Pierre—a French artist involved with Sharon when she left her husband

Richard Branson—owner of Virgin Records

Richard Tam—Chinese American fashion designer

Richard (Rick) Vick—British boyfriend of Jane Motley

Rita—early obsessive love of Judy's

Robert Browning—a retired British foreign-service officer, husband of Audrey

Rosemary Donnelly—American girlfriend of John Zervos, sister of Jim

Roshi Susaki—Buddhist monk, friend and Zen master of Leonard Cohen

Sharon—wife of Craig, whom she deserted on Hydra

Sinclair Beiles—South African poet, editor of William Burroughs' *Naked Lunch*

Skip Milson—artist and art teacher, old friend of George Lialios

Spiro—a Greek medical student from Alexandria, occasional lover of Marianne

Susan—Judy's friend in Cambridge

Suzanne—mother of Leonard's children, Adam and Lorca

Terence—a philosophy professor, lover of Rita, ex best-friend of John Taurek

Theo—Greek owner of Pyrofani's Taverna in Kamini

Valerie—wife of Brian Sidaway

Vicki Zevgolis—a Greek American houseguest of Alexis Bolens
Vickie—Australian lover of Dimitri Gassoumis
Victoria (Torie)—Judy Scott's daughter
Vibe—Vivi's partner, Danish
Vivi—Vibe's partner, Danish
Yorgo—Greek owner of the Sailing Café on the port in Hydra

INDEX